Nov 17, 1907

Mrs I. A. Linnell

Many happy returns
of the day

From David, Julia, Clarence
and Elizabeth
with love

WITHDRAWN

SAN GABRIEL—THE MOTHER MISSION

THE BETTER CITY

A SOCIOLOGICAL STUDY OF
A MODERN CITY

BY

DANA W. BARTLETT

Superintendent of the Bethlehem Institutions
Los Angeles, California

WITH ILLUSTRATIONS

LOS ANGELES
The Neuner Company Press
1907

TO MY WIFE
MY HELPMEET THROUGH MANY YEARS
OF SOCIAL SERVICE
I DEDICATE THIS BOOK

PREFACE

In the following pages a study has been made of a particular city—the one which the writer knows best—in whose welfare his life is bound up. While discussing the problems of this city, he has had a consciousness that he was discussing the problems of city life in general. For while every city has its own peculiar problems, city life in all its essential features is everywhere the same. The average modern city expresses its highest ideals in terms of greatness: Greater New York, Greater Los Angeles. It is the purpose of this book to concentrate thought upon the ethical ideal—believing that a city may become as noted for its righteousness, its morality, its social virtues, its artistic life, as for its material resources. A better city means a better country. May we each have a part in the building of The Better City.

DANA W. BARTLETT.

Los Angeles, Cal.,
Sept. 1, 1907.

Table of Contents

List of Illustrations

THE BETTER CITY

CHAPTER I.

THE CITY OF OUR LADY OF THE ANGELS

A great city is forming by the shore of the sunset sea. Great and still greater will it become as the years go by, until it stretches itself from the Sierra Madre Mountains to the Pacific. Unlike most Western cities, this City of Heart's Desire has been slow in building. Five years before the Declaration of Independence had been signed, when the great West still lay in primeval forest and its far-reaching plains were trackless and desolate, save where over them the Indians and wild animals roamed unmolested, away out by the Western waters, the Spanish padres began the planting of that wonderful line of missions along the Camino Real, or King's Highway. Then followed intrepid explorers whose purpose was to establish the Catholic faith, to extend the Spanish domain, and to check the ambitious schemes of foreign nations. In order to hold the country and give protection to the missions, presidios were established and filled with troops. But these troops must needs be supported, so agricultural colonies were brought from Mexico. One of these companies of Spanish colonists arrived at the San Gabriel Mission in 1771. The Governor had already decided to settle this little band on the rich lands along the Rio Porciuncula, now recognized as the usually dry bed of the Los Angeles River.

The actual dedication of this now historic site took place on September 4th of that year. On that morning, mass was celebrated at the mission, and the little procession took up its line of march for the site which had been chosen for the plaza of the new town. There was a parade three times around it, led by the Governor and the friars, an escort of soldiers, acolytes carrying the cross and the candles, and a woman with a banner on which was a picture of "Our Lady of the Angels," followed by the women, children and the Indians. This ceremony concluded, there was an address by the Governor, after which were volleys of musketry and the booming of a small cannon which now reposes as a curious relic of the past in a museum. According to the custom of these pious Spaniards, they christened their newborn town with a religious name—"El Pueblo de Nuestra Señora Reina de Los Angeles," "The City of Our Lady, Queen of the Angels," which succeeding generations with less time on their hands have shortened to "Los Angeles."

No sooner had the plaza, the social center,

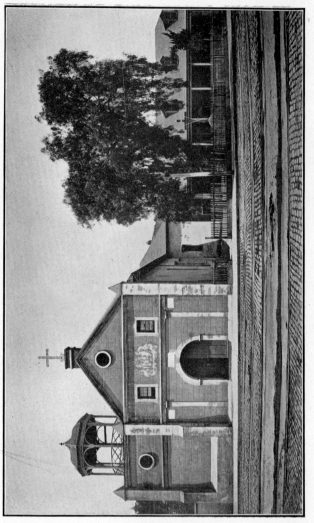

THE PLAZA CHURCH—IGLESIA DE LOS ANGELES

been laid out, than they builded hard by, the Iglesia de Los Angeles, and in these days of Eastern tourists, from a slightly different location, the bells still ring from the church tower as in the days when the señors, with their broad sombreros, walked with the black-eyed señoritas to the morning mass. But the plaza of today, near by the old site, where once centered all the social life of the pueblo, and where the music of the guitar accompanied the joyous song, is now but a well-kept park where lounge the out-of-works and those awaiting employment.

The quiet, restful pastoral life of the past furnished none of the vexed problems of the modern city life. The total population in 1790 consisted of only 141—a mixed class, composed of one European, seventy-two Spanish-Americans, seven Indians, twenty-two mulattos and thirty-nine mestizos. The large ranchos were covered with cattle. The fathers in the missions were teaching their Indians the gospel of the Prince of Peace, and at the same time training them in the cultivation of the olive and the vine. Thus the years went by without any striking event to mark their passage. The rush for gold in '49 brought the first forerunners of those who were finally to possess the land, but most of them were but birds of passage on their way to the north. The first great rush to the Land of Sunshine occurred in 1885, when in the Cajon Pass the golden

2

spike was driven which marked the completion of the Atlantic and Pacific Railroad, joining two great oceans. Following this came the great and only real estate boom, which made fortunes for the few and wrought ruin for the many. But after the dark night had passed, the citizens awakened with the determination to build here a metropolitan city, not only great, but fair and good. "Watch us grow" is the legend emblazoned today over store and along trolley lines, which extend far out into the country. Growing, yet it is conscious of its growing pains.

The beginnings of much that is to make this the better city that is to be, can be traced back to the padres, who wrought better than they knew as they introduced the mission type of architecture, so well adapted to this Southland. The mission grape, the olive, together with many flowers and vines and trees from other lands, which now beautify our city are constant reminders of those who planted them a century ago about the church, the Campo Santo, and in the acres about the sheep-fold. Unlike the frontier town, or mine-built city, this City of the Angels had as its foundation the Church, and later on, the school. These persist today in many noble institutions making constantly for the better life. The religious ideals of the first missionaries have passed on even into the nobler and truer altruistic aspirations of the present day. The power of these

ideals is still felt even though the rush for the
dollar may seem for a time to engross the minds
and hearts of many citizens. Those early dwellers in the patios taught a lesson in hospitality
which their successors have constantly put in
practice. The early traveler on the King's
Highway knew when he saw the white towers
of the mission or the tile-covered adobe on the
great rancho, that there a cordial welcome
awaited both man and beast, and that after
refreshment that cost him nothing, a guide and
a fresh horse might be his until he reached the
next stopping place, miles beyond. Is it any
wonder, then, that this and other fair sister
cities of the South should be noted as the
world's best entertainers? While today there
are some who are seeking only to obtain the
traveler's dollars, the best among us are com-
bining the old hospitality with the ability of
the modern Captain of Industry, and their
minds are filled with commercial, educational
and philanthropic schemes of largest import.

It matters not how large this city may grow,
it will never be allowed to forget the past, for
in every annual Fiesta de las Flores the early
days are again recalled. The brilliant ca-
balleros on prancing horses tell of the pleasures of old when the Spaniard in high-peaked
sombreros, and covered with silver spangles,
rode in the race, or fought "el toro" in the
ring. We are reminded of the past, too, as
we see riding by, the smiling señoritas, native

daughters of the golden West, and know that it was such as these that made this the land of poetry and romance. The cowboys riding on their ponies tell of the days when the ranchos were reckoned by leagues and not by acres, and the multitudes of cattle were raised for their hides rather than for their meat. This celebration is emphatically a Fiesta de las Flores, a feast of flowers. A multitude of the rarest blossoms entwine horse and carriage and rider in such profusion that the florists of many Eastern cities would become bankrupt if forced to supply them. At night there is the brilliant illumination of float and design, growing more and more beautiful as the years go by, but this feature of our modern electric age is one in which other cities can do as well. None other, however, can have the same background of natural beauty; none other can have the drooping peppers, the tall eucalyptus, the over-circling palms, the never-ceasing bloom of flowers, the mid-winter roses, tree-tall, and throwing forth their fragrance from ever-opening blossom, nor the golden poppy, dear to the heart of every Californian, which although much depleted by the hand of the agriculturalist, still makes our many fields one great mass of yellow bloom.

A century ago, this was the Land of Mañana. Today it is the city of the strenuous life. Yet today no one is so busy in any department of work that he does not find some time to live

THE CHINESE AND THEIR DRAGON IN FIESTA PARADE

out of doors, either by the sea, or in the heart of the mountains. This book is being written in a holy sanctuary, high up in the mother mountains, under a spreading sycamore tree, with the maple, the oak and the spruce as its companions. The walls of this nature's sanctuary are lined with ferns and moss and beautiful flowers. The squirrels and the birds in the bush are of more value than their caged fellows in the city park. The babbling of the mountain brook is nature's own medicine for tired nerves. Slow of heart, indeed, is he who cannot recognize the imminent God in the life and voices around him. It is because of the ideals of the padres which stir the newer social thought of this industrial age that the writer longs for the time to come when the workers in the mill and the toilers in the factories may in increasing numbers have the yearly opportunity of entering the silences of the mountains and there hear the still small voice that cannot be heard in the noise and rush of modern commercialism. Sooner here than anywhere else in the wide world will this dream be realized, for here all nature calls us to come out into the open and breathe the free air of heaven.

With this fair land for its setting, the City Beautiful of which we are to speak is to be built up. The story of its gradual enlargement must be told at length in another chapter. We shall now seek to indicate some of the reasons why we expect this to be a greater and a better city.

In the first place, there is the asset of climate, and there is no climate on earth equal to this, for it is enjoyable and health-giving the year around. When elsewhere men are suffering from the heat, in this favored clime the least shade is always cooling and blankets are necessary for comfort at night. When in the North and East the mercury goes down below zero, and the rivers are frozen over and the land is covered with snow, in this city men sleep with open windows, or live comfortably either in a tent house or out of doors, save in the rainy season. Here homes are built with reference to the climate, with large porches used as living rooms, with open-air bedrooms, with patios filled with blossom and rare plants —the joy of every season. Within a few miles of this city are to be found the beaches that furnish a climate cool in summer and wonderfully pleasant in winter. The mountains are near by, always enticing and invigorating, and in the winter furnish the touch of snow for those who desire the chill, so that they may experience again the crisp air of their old home winter. Thousands of children and youths in this city have never seen snow nearer than the distant mountain tops, and yet this is not an ennervating climate. It is unlike the tropics, where because of the excessive moisture and heat, men are content to sit down under the bread-fruit tree and live without much labor. Here with the air charged with electricity and ozone, there is a bracing quality that makes the sick well and the strong capable of doing hard work without great exhaustion.

Climate has a cash value. It is the climate that brings hither three-fourths of the tourists, and leads the majority to stay after they have spent a winter where none of the rigors of winter weather are experienced. This is a national playground. The rich from all over the world are coming hither on pleasure bent. Nearly every day is a fine day, and life may be one round of joy. Hither comes not only the invalid, but the man of business that he may find the quiet and peaceful closing of a happy life. A recent writer, enthusiastic, yet keeping well within bounds, says: "Here is the climate of the tropics without its perils; here is the fertility of Egypt without its fellaheen; here are the fruits and flowers of Sicily without its lazzaroni; here the beauty of Italy without its limited market; the sunshine of Persia without its oppressions. For this is America, with its unfettered freedom and unfettered energy."

But to none has the climate such a cash value as to the working man. No days lost because of the storm or cold; no using up in winter of that which has been saved in summer; no suffering from lack of coal or clothing. On the other hand, he is able to possess a home of his own, and though its walls may be only the thickness of a single board, yet covered with flowers and vines, it equals in comfort an Eastern palace. In this clime the rancher sees many of his crops grow continuously, and is able to reap in winter as well as in summer. In such a climate the struggle for existence will always be modified, and can never under the worst conditions be like that of other cities.

This climate has its sociological bearing on the housing problem—for here the tendency is to open and not to crowded quarters; on morality, for those who cultivate a taste for natural pleasures are not tempted to the grosser sins. Here even the pauper lives in surroundings fit for a king. It has its bearing on health. Every sensible doctor will recommend the "open-air cure" as the most effectual remedy for nearly every disease. And here there are more perfect days during the year for out-of-door life, than are to be found anywhere else. Plenty of fresh air with absence of worry, peace of mind and some definite object in life will surely bring health to any of God's creatures.

Another reason why Los Angeles is to be not only a greater but a better city, is found in the fact that it is largely an American city. The majority of its citizens are of American birth; and its foreign-born citizen, catching the American spirit, vies with his neighbor in his devotion to high ideals. The people of culture have come from every point of the compass to make up the present city of nearly

A SPANISH HOME GATHERING

IN THE OLD PUEBLO DAYS

300,000 and to join with the old settlers in planning for a greater city with a million happy citizens. The amalgamation of races is producing a new and splendid type. Here is a people within whose veins runs the red blood of the hardy Northmen. They are possessed of the push and the stir of the great Eastern cities, and have also the romantic and poetic temperament of the Spanish life in which they share, together with the love of nature and of the beautiful that characterized the early settlers. The out-of-door life, the mission residence, the bungalow, are but the outward expression of the inner thought. Here as in no other city, you can hear the song of the siren mingled with the music of mission bells.

The greatness, at least of the City of the Angels can be prophesied because its commercial prospects are brighter than ever before. With three great transcontinental lines and the coming of the fourth, with a harbor in the making that will cost the Government about $4,000,000, with mighty steamships carrying the product of a thousand factories to the teeming millions of the Orient, what can stop this city from becoming one of the great commercial centers of the earth? This city has acquired water rights in the high Sierras that will make it possible to bring from the Owens River in a conduit two hundred and fifty miles long, water sufficient for a city of two millions. In a land where water means so much and where it has the power to transform the desert into a garden, who can picture the beauty and greatness of the future City of the Angels, when this gigantic scheme becomes an accomplished fact?

The first city in the Union to light its streets entirely with electricity, Los Angeles is now one of the best lighted cities in all the land. To one standing on the surrounding mountain tops, the city presents a brilliant appearance with numerous high masts carrying groups of lights, and with the many thousand electric globes marking the streets in every direction. With several of the principal streets lighted by clusters of lights on ornamental iron electroliers, the city seems as though prepared for a perpetual fiesta.

It is easy to become enthused as to the possible greatness of a growing city. While the aim of this book is ethical rather than historical, the author describes the Greater Los Angeles with the hope that there may be awakened an equal enthusiasm regarding the Better Los Angeles. Long years ago this city outgrew the cactus-hedged boundaries of the old pueblo, and now the cry is for a city from the mountains to the sea. Even at the present this is more than a dream, for beginning at Altadena in the foothills, there is hardly a break as the traveler descends by trolley through Pasadena—the Queen of the Valley—South Pasadena, Garvanza, Highland Park, and on through the city itself, toward Long Beach. In the seaward direction, the workingmen own thousands of homes. Compton almost touches the last tract laid out by the Long Beach promoter. Going toward the west, Hollywood, Sherman and the Soldiers' Home almost reach that wonderful line of beach resorts extending from Playa del Rey to Santa Monica. In view of this wonderful development, the city has already appointed a committee which has reported favorably on a plan for the consolidation of city and county, by constituting nine boroughs, reaching from San Fernando to San Pedro, and from San Gabriel to the ocean front. At a recent election, a narrow strip of land reaching from the city limits to Wilmington and San Pedro was annexed, thus making it possible to reach tide water where Los Angeles can own its own harbor.

At present there are about 780 miles of streets; and there are plans on foot for the building of a poppy-lined boulevard from Pasadena to the city, continuing it to Long Beach in the Pacific Boulevard, and toward the western sea by an extension of the Sunset Boulevard along the foothill section of the Cahuenga Valley. A kite-shaped boulevard is projected toward the east, touching all the towns in both directions to Redlands and Riverside. In view of all this, together with the development of the rapid transit system—a system already far ahead of other cities, it is small wonder that the mind becomes some-what intoxicated with the sense of evident destiny.

But it is well to remember that the desire for mere wealth and outward greatness has proved the ruin of many a city. The quest for the dollar blinds the eyes to the higher civic ideals. The fact is, that city life had its Dark Age until the beginning, but a few years ago, of the Civic Renaissance. Then came the "ten years' war" against the slum, made necessary by forty years of neglect and lack of civic self-sacrifice. Graft and misrule in the city hall have only recently been met with high business ideals, and the reapplication of the phrase, "a public office, a public trust."

During the past fifteen years the social workers and the public press have gradually evolved a new patriotism. The social conscience of many has been aroused, and a feeling of community obligation and purpose is possessing many who once lived only the life of selfish commercialism. There has been many a signal victory of right ideals in these last few years. Frederick Howe in the Outlook gives a notable example: "In a few years' time the Cleveland Chamber of Commerce has compelled its members to think about the city in a city way, and today its members talk not so much about bank clearances, tonnage, freight rates, and business for their own personal profit; they talk city, street cleaning, health protection, parks, public baths, schools, model tenements, cheap light, heat, and transportation for all the people. The work is not all done yet, and the commercial impulse is keenly alert when its business interests are involved. But the Chamber has got its bent, and it can never become again a mere temple of money makers."

Los Angeles has been lavishly endowed by Nature with all that goes to make up a prosperous city, and commercially its future is secured. But greatness is not necessarily goodness; indeed, it may be its greatest foe. Is it not then an opportune time to lay emphasis on the Better City, setting forth high ideals as to private virtue and honesty, high ideals as to industrial and civic life, so that the better city may be created for the benefit and enjoyment of all the people?

The writer, after many years spent as a social worker in this city, can testify to the great awakening along all social lines today. Everywhere, among rich and poor alike, there seems to be a deep purpose to make this city not alone greater, but pre-eminently "better, wiser, and fairer."

As this is written the Landmarks Club is preparing to rehabilitate the old missions, planted so long ago amid privation and suffering on the part of the padres. Before long the traveler along the rebuilt Camino Real will be able to pause under the arches of the mission, while the brown-robed Franciscan bids him enter; and in the stillness of its cloisters he will be invited to think of those things that are eternal and abiding, and which make for the true greatness of all human life. Visions, dreams, ideals, they also have a part in the making of the Better City.

CHAPTER II.

THE CITY BEAUTIFUL

Ugliness has no commercial or ethical value. The crowded tenement, the rookery, a city's ill-kept streets and yards are not incentives to higher living. On the other hand, it is a fact made clear by years of experience that the fairer the city, the nearer to Nature's heart the people are brought; the more easily they are governed; there is less crime and more of the normal, spiritual, healthful life which is the product of the ripest civilization.

The last half century has seen a rapid development of factory and commercial life. Will it pay large dividends? has been the only question asked in the building of store or mill. The busy strenuous life has left little time for the study of the beautiful. But new times are upon us. The artist and the artisan, the teacher and the merchant, the social dreamer and the social worker, each in his own way, has plans for the City Beautiful. It is a sign of great promise when the daily papers, usually so filled with commercialism, partisan politics, and with the shadier side of life are giving so much attention to the aesthetic and artistic side of a city's development. One of our city papers devotes a page a week to this subject, under a well-trained editor. Every city paper prints a strong succession of editorials on beautifying the city, and these editorials are generally untainted with utilitarian ideas. Recently a Pasadena editor wrote in answer to the question, "What is beauty?": "It is the embodiment of truth in visible forms, and ugliness is the assertion of a lie. The love of the beautiful is but the hungry human nature feeling after infinite harmony. Everywhere in literature, in art, in being, the beautiful is the true, and yet we pursue the ugly, believing the beautiful too costly. We permit it for a few dollars gained or a few dollars saved, and think how well it pays. But sometime, the right to banish the ugly, simply because it is the ugly—which is now denied by the courts— will be recognized. The children of the earth must come into their full heritage, and when they do, we shall see how natural is beauty; how near to simplicity; how much it consists simply in retaining unspoiled the things of nature and of life."

What has been done along this line in the past, is well worthy of study. Every New Englander will recall the many towns like New Haven, where the century-old elms form charming vistas down all the streets; where the Commons furnishes the site for the church, the town hall, and perhaps for the school, thus becoming the forerunner of the modern idea of a civic center for the City

THE PLAZA

Beautiful. The early days were days of high ideals, but our land soon fell on evil times. Greed, fraud and incompetency vaulted into the saddle, the best men of the community being too busy, or too ignorant of existing conditions, to care for things that did not seem to be vital.

But at last the iconoclast is abroad. Parties and institutions are being battered on all sides. Necessary as this may be, there is far more need in the present hour for men of positive thought and high ideals — constructive men who are able to do something worth doing. Holding to the thought of the high and the beautiful is the quickest way of overthrowing the false and the unlovely. The dreamer, the idealist—the one who is under the power of a great ideal, is of more value than he who fights in Saul's armor. Every Utopia has its Moore, or its Bellamy. Inspired by their vision, the opportunist begins his slow work in the midst of the actual conditions toward the Utopia which lies far beyond.

This City of the Angels can be among the first to realize the world's dream of the City Beautiful, for all the materials are at hand in such an abundance that everything can be easily transformed. The very outbuildings and fences run riot with glorious climbers, Cherokee roses, passion vines and nasturtiums, and the porches are intertwined with yellow and white banksias. For the yards and the

3

streets, there is a choice of a score of trees, rarely seen in the East—oranges, magnolias, palms, peppers, camphors, laurels, live oaks, and the scarlet-blooming eucalyptus. Trees are here from every clime, as can easily be seen in Chaves Ravine in Elysian Park, where there are over thirty acres of propagated plants and vines, seen elsewhere only in hothouses. Here, with its wealth of purple bloom, is the largest bougainvillea in the world. Running along a trellis for more than 200 feet, this gigantic creeper has stretched itself in a prodigality of intertwining tendril and leaf. An Empress of China rose has attained a growth of 150 feet. The possibilities in the growth of vine arbors are seen in the many creeping plants of strange variety.

In the past, through false ideas of mere political office holders, cement sidewalks and curbs, electric poles and gridiron streets were thought to be of more civic value than the stately trees planted by the early settlers. So the woodman used his ax, and years were lost in the effort to make this a forest city—a place that will fulfill the vision of William Morris, of the time "when art will make our streets as beautiful as the woods and as elevating as the mountain sides; when it will be a pleasure and a rest, and not a weight upon the spirit to come from the open country into the city."

The proper planting of street trees means so much to the city as a whole, that the munici-

pality has placed the matter under the control
of a Tree Warden, that he may determine the
kind, usually planting whole streets with uni-
formity—and give constant attention to the
care and trimming of trees, in order that there
may be no break in the arboreal effect. Already Ward Improvement Societies have undertaken the uniform planting of trees in their
localities, thereby enhancing the beauty of the
ward, and the value of the property. The
old way of planting gave, here an acacia, there
a palm, there a pepper, with an intervening
treeless lot, losing thereby the opportunity
for an artistic effect. Real estate agents, laying out new subdivisions whose streets are to
be deeded to the city, ought not to be allowed
to plant trees, except under the direction of the
city Tree Warden.

The laying out of the streets is by no means
to be overlooked in the City Beautiful. Philadelphia's checkerboard plan has unfortunately
been followed in this city, and the hills have
been cut through by cañons in order to extend
the streets, and they who live on the hills are
modern cliff dwellers. Better, Boston with its
crooked streets, of which a humorist was heard
to say that in following a single street he often
met himself coming in the opposite direction.
Many new subdivisions have, however,
adopted the more excellent plan of having the
streets laid out with reference to the contour
of the hills, built through ornamental parks

and beside winding paths, and leading to the mission homes and bungalows which crown the summit.

Opportunities for making the City Beautiful are far greater here than in other cities built on the level ground, or lacking the nearby mountain views. The City of the Angels is beautiful for situation, lying as it does at the very base of the Sierra Madre Mountains. Between the foothills, to the north and east of the city, there are many valleys, such as those of San Fernando, Eagle Rock, San Gabriel, filled with choice towns, destined one day to be part of the greater city. The hills reaching into the very heart of Los Angeles furnish most sightly places for beautiful houses and magnificent hotels. Some of our country's greatest tourist hotels are now being built upon the hilltops, thus making it possible for the traveler to avoid the brick-built, noisy hostelry in the midst of the city's commercial life.

The city is divided into two parts by the Los Angeles River, the high east bank receding in a rolling mesa, while on the more level ground to the west, lies the business district of the city. Breaking through the range of hills in the north, the river throughout its entire length can be made into a line of beauty. Entering the river from the Pasadena side, is the Arroyo Seco, a stream whose bed is dry in summer but which in winter carries quite a volume of water. This is bordered with a natural growth of trees and shrubs, live oaks and sycamores. Along this can be made one of the most charming drives that any city could desire. Although almost in the heart of the greater Los Angeles, the Arroyo has the effect of silence and beauty of the forest and mountain, and along its banks are built some of the most unique and costly dwellings of the Southland.

Señor Dominguez, of the great Dominguez rancho, was the first dreamer of the Greater Los Angeles, as thirty years ago he prophesied "one city from the mountains to the sea." If that lover of poetry and romance could return today and stand upon the banks of the Los Angeles River, much like other rivers, save in the quality of its wave reflection, he would find it possessing still all its ancient possibilities of beauty and adornment, despite the fact that its banks are lined with factories and the river bed itself is sought by utilitarian corporations. He might say with the poet Campbell, who returned to his beloved Clyde, and found it thus defiled:

"And call they this improvement?—to have changed
My native Clyde, thy once romantic shore,
Where Nature's face is banished and estranged
And Heaven reflected in thy wave no more."

Think of what value to the city this river might yet become if placed under a special commission empowered to carry out a definite plan for its reclamation from base uses. The river should be crossed by ornamental bridges, each a work of art; beneath the bridges and above the water line, should be the city-owned tracks for both steam and electric railways. On either side should be an esplanade with park effects, and wide driveways for automobiles and carriages, with a pleasant promenade beautifully lighted at night by light clusters on ornamental posts, forming a natural boulevard that might reach even to the sea. The bordering factories and warehouses should be hidden behind a wealth of climbing vines and roses. The land for the new civic centers in Chicago cost that city many millions, but by using this river bed, such centers can be built at very small cost. We would suggest the following plan: Let the river bed from First Street north to Elysian Park be cleaned of all rubbish and undergrowth, the sand hills leveled, thus making, during nine months of the year, an extensive playground for the children of the congested districts. On a level with the bridges there could be built, on piers, three civic centers with halls for lectures and entertainments, club rooms, baths and gymnasium, with steps leading down to the riverbed playground. Treated according to such a plan, the river bed may add much to the making of the City Beautiful. And yet to think that only a few months ago, this river with all its latent possibilities, was almost given away to a railroad corporation, by a Council which did not realize its value to the city.

No one can speak of the beautiful in Los Angeles without including the mother mountains that are so near. Any scheme for beautifying the city must be formed with reference to this wonderful background. Think of the cool refreshing cañons, within easy reach of rich and poor alike, by trolley or by drive— Santa Monica Cañon, Cahuenga Pass the cañons of Verdugo, Millard, Eaton, Santa Anita and San Gabriel. In two hours by trolley, incline and burro to the top of Mt. Lowe; in five hours by trolley and burro, an easy journey to the summit of Mt. Wilson, overlooking to the south the Pacific Coast, and to the north, Pine Mountain, Strawberry Peak, Barley Flats, West Fork, and on to the far Pacific Mountain and Mt. Emma—an inspiring sight, never to be forgotten. The tourist who does not make this journey has not seen the real unchanging California, with its primeval forests untouched by man.

Because of their very nearness to the city's heart, working men and their families, in increasing numbers are making their way to the mountain tops. Many walk, some carry their blankets and sleep under the stars; others with dollars in their pockets to pay all expenses, enjoy all the luxuries of a modern hotel. Last night, the writer, surrounded by his family, slept on a mountain in the open.

Awakened by the rising of the full-orbed moon, he saw the smaller stars put to sleep by the brighter light, and only the larger constellations remained to add their part to the brilliancy of the night. The light and shadow of tree and rock, the undulating but softened sky-line presented a picture for an artist. The voices of the night made only sufficient discord to bring out the harmony of the strange concert of God's little creatures. As dawn came on, the songs of the birds were a reminder of the saying of St. Francis when the birds came about him in the mountains, "I believe, dearest brethren, that our Lord is pleased that we should dwell on this solitary mount, inasmuch as our brothers and sisters, the birds, show such joy at our coming." It will do you good, my friend, if you can for a few days, or better still for a few weeks, dwell in this wonderful land of Mañana, where the cares of today do not press, and tomorrow seems a long way off. Journeying to the mountain tops, you at last stand in the presence of the Great Spirit. For the first time, it may be, your soul seems to be at one with the divine. Everything is in tune with the infinite. The rising sun, tipping with gold the eastern mountains, is the herald of a new day; the wondrous reach of mountains, rolling range on range into the almost infinite distance; the giants of the forest, centuries old; the birds, vari-colored and tuneful—are not these works of a creator, each one speaking His

IN THE MOTHER MOUNTAINS

Presence in a voice both musical and sublime? Drink in here of God's strength. It was with you when you were in the midst of toil; when with continuous struggle you were trying to cast out demons, but knew not where to find the power. There is so little in a great city that speaks of the spiritual, but on the mountain top it seems to press in at every pore. You can draw it in at every breath. You can dip down deep into the great ocean of spiritual power and be made strong. The writer longs for such changes in our economic life, that all the city workers may have this opportunity of becoming acquainted with "our brothers and sisters, the birds," and receive this mountain-top inspiration for the better life.

Is it necessary that all this inspiration be lost on the return to the artificiality of city life? Must it evaporate when we again touch the city, with its brick and mortar, its steel and cement, its hypocrisies and false living? Many of the city's noblest souls are saying that this is not necessary. The New Los Angeles can be made a place of inspiration for nobler living, and to this end many are working in church and settlement, in Woman's Club and Civic League. On the lowest plane, they are teaching those who cannot understand values unless expressed in dollars, that beauty pays. That is why the railroads give so much attention to the beautifying of their stations, often maintaining extensive greenhouses and em-

ploying expert florists and landscape garden-
ers. The Huntington trolley lines are bordered by poppy-lined boulevards. Replacing
the old plan of taking the travelers through
back yards and dropping them down in the
midst of low groggeries, is the newer plan of
landing them in a beautiful and stately station
in the midst of a flower garden, surrounded
by the city's most imposing buildings. It
surely pays to give the impression that here are
citizens with high standards of living and
noble purposes—and first impressions are last-
ing. "Pray, Sir Mercury, why ridest thou in
so fine a chariot, when thy winged sandals will
save both thy time and birds, too?" "It is to
show," quoth the god, "an example to mortals
who in their daily affairs ought not to forget
that their business can best be served by
beauty."

And if beauty pays, there is still a higher
reason for the making of the City Beautiful—
namely, the bearing of beauty upon morality.
To appeal to the sense of beauty takes the
mind away from the artificial and fixes it upon
the real; it softens the business man in his
competitive struggle and gives him something
better worth doing than crushing his less fortunate brethren; it brings all men to that place
where they can recognize themselves as crea-
tors—as sons of God—and feel a power moving
within them, which before was lying dormant;
it gives the society woman something better

to think of than parties and dress; it is calculated to produce a new generation of large-hearted, philanthropic, altruistic women, of which the world will be justly proud.

Healthful conditions of living, an unsurpassed climate, a wealth of bloom and foliage, with unlimited room for expansion, have brought hither many wealthy and cultured families. Pasadena, Los Angeles' ideal suburb, is the home of many millionaires, who have built beautiful homes surrounded by private parks—the delight of all eastern visitors. Still nearer is Hollywood, the home of de Longpre, the flower artist, which no one should visit the city without seeing. During the past year, one of the merchants has created grounds equal to those of an ancient palace, by buying many rare old trees from old-time home places, now being covered with business blocks. In this way he will have grounds of surpassing beauty which it would otherwise have taken more than a quarter of a century to acquire.

William Morris taught that "it is the business of each of us to build and adorn a house for our own physical and social comfort and our artistic joy." In Southern California as nowhere else are found the conditions making this easy of accomplishment. Here much thought and attention are given to home building, and the leading architects of the city are giving of their best efforts to the production of charming houses. And no commission will tempt them to reproduce the style of house another man has paid for. That is his home, and he alone has a right to the plans. This has produced a city of many styles and kinds of architecture, the mission predominating because of its adaptability to the climate. Here are to be seen wide, overhanging eaves and cornices, with patios and loggias; back yards beautifully decorated with flowers and vines, so as to constitute the real outdoor living rooms. "The exterior of your home," said Ruskin, "is not private property." That which can be seen from the streets is the real concern of the neighbors and the city at large. The architecture of the home, the decoration of the grounds is each man's contribution to the City Beautiful, and one way in which he can give pleasure and enjoyment to the people.

A very great addition to the City Beautiful is made by the great sweep of ocean on the south and west of the Greater City. The old resorts of Santa Monica, Redondo, San Pedro and Long Beach are now reënforced by many artistically laid out towns within reach of all parts of Los Angeles, by easy and rapid transit. Venice and Naples are laid out with canals and stately homes, with such building restrictions that will guarantee perpetual home sites for all who build. For a fare of fifty cents, anyone can spend a delightful day on the beach, and the cost of a week's vacation is not so great as to preclude working men and their families from having an opportunity for such an outing.

The effect of beauty upon the children is receiving much attention. The days of the three R's are nearly past, and through nature study and school gardens, thousands of girls and boys are receiving an ideal education, growing daily stronger, happier and better. Greek and Calculus are no doubt necessary for the fullest development of the mind, but the boy and girl are better prepared for the higher studies, if in the lower grades they have been brought into sympathetic contact with the simpler things of the life around them. "The real aim of such education is to cultivate close observation of plant life, to instill a deep love for plant culture, and by so doing awaken the young student to the refining influence of plants in the school and in the home, and to enable them to be an inspiration to others from the fullness of their pleasure in the work." Persian boys, twenty centuries ago, received practical instruction in horticulture, and for years school gardens have existed on the Continent.

In America, this movement for bringing city children near to Nature's heart was begun by Mr. Henry Lincoln Clapp in 1890, at a Boy's Grammar School in Boston. Here wild flowers and ferns were raised, and ten years later a kitchen garden was added. Small school gardens in school yards were slowly undertaken in other cities. From 1902, until the present, the movement has gone on with increasing interest, alike on the part of the teacher and pupils. When Mrs. Henry Parsons succeeded in transforming that tract of land in New York, covered with debris and tumbledown houses, known as "Hell's Kitchen," and by the aid of the boys and girls made it a most beautiful garden, tended by a happy class of orderly children, she was not raising vegetables alone, but was training souls in the things that are of abiding value. In every city of our land is now found the school garden, within the school ground, on city-owned land, or on vacant lots. In and out of the school hours, the child is kept off the street and placed in a fairy land of living green. Said Helen C. Bennett, "The plants are his children; he sows the seed, watches its birth and helps its growth. Gardens do more than train the hands and head; they touch and awaken the soul." Correlated with indoor studies, these outdoor studies make almost alive such exercise as reading, language, spelling, arithmetic, bookkeeping, drawing, geography and history. The relation of this new movement to the City Beautiful can be seen at a glance. Whenever gardens are established and prize packets of seeds are sold to the pupils, backyard cultivation begins, sanitary conditions are improved, piles of dirt and rubbish disappear, peas, beans, lettuce and bright flowers take their place, and the City Beautiful begins to emerge into view. The call for teachers for the school gardens has created a new profession, and already normal schools are responding to the demand with special courses. In Porto Rico, the United States Government regularly trains teachers for this work, in a course comprising theoretical and practical lessons in agriculture, and places a trained teacher in a garden for every school.

One great trouble in this and other cities, is the lack of land for the purpose. But there are many ill-kept lots, whose owners might be persuaded to loan them to the school board, while waiting for an increase in value, thus improving the appearance of the city and the character of the children at the same time.

In Los Angeles much has been done in a local way by Ward Improvement Associations. Some years ago, the Eighth Ward Association, in the most congested part of the city, placed the following circular in every home, with excellent results: "Neighbors, let us coöperate that we may have clean streets and sidewalks, front and rear yards beautified, and healthy surroundings for our children. To this end, let us see that the street in front of the residence is kept clean from paper, tins and all kinds of rubbish. Put cans, bones, ashes in a separate receptacle and place out on garbage days. Teach the children never to throw garbage in the street. It is unsightly, and may be unhealthy. Sweep the sidewalks whenever necessary. Report all cases of broken sinks and closets to the health office, provided the owner will not fix them. Let us beautify our yards. In this wonderful climate, where flowers grow so readily, we may have gardens which would be the pride of the rich in the East. Prepare front yards and back yards if possible; fertilize and plant seeds and vines. The association will gladly donate the seeds and cuttings. The growth of potted plants for porches and windows is recommended. Neighbors, let us coöperate."

No scheme for beautifying the city can be complete that does not include a comprehensive plan for a metropolitan park system. We have scarcely begun to plan for the noiseless city, but are content to allow nerve-racking, unnecessary noises. We join the rush as though there was no time for else but business. We wear out before our time. The park offers the opportunity to escape from the noises and associations of the city, and in touch with Nature, to find repose for mind and body. "The parks are the lungs of the city. They are the sanitariums for the people who cannot afford to hie themselves to the country or seaside. They give sunlight and green fields free of cost. They are the civilizers and equalizers for the poor."

In England the Commons were gradually wrested from the people by the nobles, and until the past fifty years, the people have had

IN A LOS ANGELES PARK

very little of what could be called common
land. Kings and nobles held the great deer
runs and forests and natural parks as their
own, and if a common man was caught poach-
ing, he could be banished across the seas. But
times have changed and London has its 13,000
acres of public parks, and 1,200 acres of private
parks. The names are familiar to all—Hyde
Park, from the old manor of Hyde, is 400 acres
in extent; Victoria Park, of 300 acres; Ham-
stead Heath, of 240 acres; Regent's Park, of
450 acres; Kensington Gardens, once a king's
palace, of 290 acres. Paris has nearly 90,000
acres devoted to public parks, the parks of
France being pieces of primeval forests pre-
served from the days of Julius Cæsar. In
America many cities have parks that have
cost them millions of dollars to acquire, and
yet they have felt that it was money well invested. If the cities had awakened earlier to
the value of their beauty spots, for how much
less might this land have been obtained!

In proportion to its population, Los Angeles
ranks well in the size of its parks. Yet seeing
we all believe that this city is soon to have a
million inhabitants, now is the time to preëmpt
more land for parks, both large and small.
For instance, in the foothills and mountains
there are many small but beautiful cañons,
now privately owned, that ought to be acquired
to serve as pleasure ground for the larger city.
Some part of the ocean front should be re-

4

served for great seaside parks, for all time. The perpetual use of the Sierra Madres as a pleasure resort has been guaranteed to the city by the Government, through the withdrawal from the market of the hundreds of miles of mountains, making them a timber reserve, which is as sacred as a National Park.

What more can be done with the present park area of this city? Excepting Elysian and Griffith Park, all are now under a high state of cultivation, filled with choice shrubs, trees and flowers—things of grace and beauty—with lakes, boats, swans, seals, animals and birds, a study ground in botany and zoology for every child in school. Outside of a few small parks, the present demand is not for more elaborate landscape gardening, but for larger tracts of land, where the underbrush is cleared only in part, and there is the natural condition which the city dweller longs for; parks so large that there is room for the planting of all kinds of trees in their native soils and altitudes. Los Angeles has two such parks. Elysian Park, one of these, contains 500 acres, and is the remnant of thousands of acres once owned by the city. Lying in the frostless belt, almost any tropical growth can be made to flourish there. It is in the south bend of the Los Angeles River, and from its highest point is to be seen a panorama of mountain, hill and valley, grand and beautiful. As yet this valuable ground, save in its botanical gardens, is cultivated only at the entrance of Fremont Gate.

The beautiful Fairmont Park in Philadelphia, costing the city $9,000,000, is said to be worth $175,000,000. What then will be the value, a quarter of a century hence of Griffith Park, the other of our extensive parks, and the largest park site of any city, having over 3,000 acres of hill and valley, with cactus slopes and wooded dale? This park, the gift of Mr. Griffith, is now far from the city, and as yet without adequate drives and approaches. The National Government has offered to grant many trees each year for the proper planting of the hillsides. The best possible plan for the forming of an up-to-date park should be made by competent engineers, and worked out year by year, as money is available. Los Angeles as yet scarcely realizes the value of this gift. Dr. W. A. Lamb, formerly of the Park Commission, makes a valuable suggestion that should be followed: "We should ask the legislature to create a non-political park commission to take up the work of amplifying; also ask that the Supreme Court be vested with the power of creating a treasury board, these two bodies to act jointly as custodians of any property that might be donated to the State for civic improvement. We want to make it easy for our wealthy citizens to contribute to the public's pleasure and comfort."

But it is not enough that citizens are interested in sections of their own city. The present demand is for a comprehensive plan of beautifying buildings covering not only the present city, but reaching far out into the suburbs. There has been a rapid growth of this new idea. Already there are over 800 associations in various parts of the land, working for the City Beautiful. This demand has created a new profession—that of the city architect, beauty expert, or civic decorator—a profession so unique that the title has not yet become fixed. There are a few leaders of national repute, such as Frederick Law Olmstead, Daniel Burnham and Charles M. Robinson, who are rapidly making a name for themselves. Many young men in school will no doubt choose this profession and become leaders in the creation of the newer cities of the future, and in the rebuilding of older ones. Far ahead of their time were George Washington and Major L'Enfant, who laid out the plans for the Capital City in 1791. Much of their plan, too great for their successors, was spoiled in the development, yet a late commission has been given power to carry out the group scheme of building in making the new Washington.

Under Olmstead's direction, Kansas City has begun its fight for beauty. Perhaps the most notable plan is that of Olmstead for the grouping of public buildings in Cleveland, remaking the city according to a definite plan.

Although costing many millions, the people of Cleveland have decided on making the city over according to the new idea. A wonderful city will be the result.

Three years ago public-spirited citizens in San Francisco, imbued by a new spirit of civic adornment, founded the "Association for the Improvement and Adornment of San Francisco," with James D. Phelan, ex-mayor, as president. They immediately employed Mr. Burnham to draw plans for the City Beautiful by the Golden Gate. He and his assistants, seated in their bungalow on Twin Peaks wrought out a plan such as would have made this the Naples of the New World, a plan so large, and requiring so many changes in streets and buildings, that as Burnham said, to work it out in its fullness would have taken more years than we live, and more millions perhaps that than we can guess. But a dire calamity fell upon that city. Undaunted, Mr. Phelan called for the architect to return, to tell them what could be done with a city in ruin. Again a plan was drawn with widened streets, a civic center, terraced hilltops, boulevards, parks, an amphitheater, a gigantic acropolis, and so on in mighty proportions. God grant that somehow, at some time, this dream of Daniel Burnham's may yet come true, and that this sea-locked city may rise from its great misfortune and be a better, fairer and wiser city, a place beautiful to behold, where the children of men will be glad to call themselves the followers of the humble St. Francis.

But Los Angeles with much of natural beauty, also needs a city plan that the best results may be secured. The Municipal Art Commission has invited a city architect to aid us. When he comes it will be well, if like Mr. Burnham on the Twin Peaks, he could live on the summit of one of the nearby mountains, until there should come to him the mighty vision of the "City of our Lady of the Angels," wrought out into the City Beautiful, with mountain, foothills, river, hilltops, seashore, parks, boulevards, happy homes—with the prodigality of nature overmantling all—and when that vision should find embodiment in a definite plan, no true son of this Southland would fail to give the plan endorsement and support, even though it might cost millions to fulfill the dream. It will pay well to make this the City Beautiful, inasmuch as that will go far toward making it the Better City.

CHAPTER III.

CIVIC BETTERMENT

All cities have gone wrong. Graft and misrule have corrupted politics. The saloon, the gambling hell, the house of ill-fame, have debauched the young and wrecked the lives of thousands. Because there was money to be made by building tenements, multitudes of children have been cursed rather than born into the world. By exploiting the labor of women and children, lives have been blighted and a false standard of living created. The corporation and the trust are able, because of their vast resources, to escape taxation and to secure laws favorable to their interests. Self-interest has been taking for itself that which belongs to the people. All through the years, organized religion has been seeking to better conditions largely through reaching the individual. Los Angeles is a city of churches, closely banded together in their work for humanity's uplift. The schools are super-excellent in teaching force, in buildings and in advanced methods. Its citizens, gathered from every quarter, are of a high class. All these it has, and yet it has missed the mark. Within the last few years, unselfishness, in its efforts to restrain organized selfishness, has itself become organized, much to the discomfiture of the mercenaries who have controlled the government and pocketed the gains. There must in the future be no less work for individual betterment, but upon a right understanding of the social obligations is where the emphasis is to be laid. The children in their schools, the mothers in their congresses, the women in their clubs, the voters in their leagues, the ministers and the laymen in their conventions, are with high civic ideals working with grim determination to make the City of the Angels a better place in which to live.

The best citizens are now no longer money makers and spenders only, but they are interested in playgrounds and baths; in coffee clubs, and men's hotels; in vacation schools; and school gardens; in university extension courses and in social settlements; in improvement associations and in adornment commissions; in the new charity and in the new patriotism; in the housing problem; in sanitation; in health and in morals; in anti-saloon measures and in saloon substitutes; in law enactment and in law enforcement; in fact in civic betterment in all its phases. With an increasing number of the best citizens, the interest is not so much in exploiting real estate as in the development of true citizenship. The Non-partisan in city government is altruistic. The Women's Club is practical in its methods of work, dealing with billboards and garbage, municipal art

A TYPICAL LOS ANGELES STREET

and ornamental bridges, the Juvenile Court and the Detention Home, the noiseless City, and the City Beautiful.

The organized movements for civic betterment have become specialized in various clubs and leagues. The Chamber of Commerce, one of the largest organizations of its kind in the world, devotes its attention to the furtherance of the interests of Los Angeles, advertising its commercial advantages throughout the East, and locally aiding such movements as are calculated to increase its desirability as a place of residence or business. It keeps a close watch on corporations seeking their own selfish interests rather than the larger ends of the community. The creation of public opinion through its various committees, in regard to such matters as roads, and boulevards, is no small part of its activities.

The Municipal League is a body of over 600 prominent citizens, joined for the purpose of better government. While acting as a general detective agency in discovering wrong and in following up evil doers, its chief work is constructive, standing as it does for the establishment of the highest type of civic government. To stimulate interest in the subject of civic beauty, the Secretary of the League gives stereopticon lectures before churches and Improvement Associations. Because of the rapid growth of the city and the great issues to come before the municipality; such as the Owen's

River water system; the consolidation question; and the great civic improvement propositions; this League has a wide field of usefulness before it, especially along the line of suggestion, for "the contagion of suggestion" applies to the good as well as to the bad. The question of better streets has been promoted by this organization. It believes that outside of the paved area the best results can be obtained by the adoption of what is known as the petrolithic method. This method which was worked out first in Santa Monica gives a road which is said to be near perfection. The street is harrowed up and the oil mixed with dirt until a paste is made. This is then tamped down by machinery until it is almost as hard as an asphalt street. The cost of this type of road is $3,000 a mile, and it does not need repairing for seven years.

It is this newly awakened interest in such practical details on the part of the leading citizens that affords ground for an optimistic view of the city's future. Let us hope that never again shall this city backslide because its citizens are too busy about their individual affairs to detect the evil and to suggest and labor for the good.

The Merchants and Manufacturers Association is an organization of business men which devotes its attention to guarding the business activities of the city against fraud. It is largely due to the work of this Asso-

ciation that the annual celebrations of the
Fiesta de las Flores are so much of a success,
as they are under the direction of that organization.

The three largest organizations of men are
often called upon to suggest methods of action
for the city officials, or for advice regarding
any great question when there is not the time
or the money to refer it to the people.

Another group of men, joined together for
the purpose of bettering existing conditions,
and which has done much in the past, is the
Voter's League. Owing to the speed at which
the powerful trolley cars are run in the city,
and the utter inadequacy of the fenders with
which these cars were provided, a large number
of accidents and deaths was the inevitable result. The Voter's League took under consideration the rectification of both these matters. Booths were erected on the street corners
and the signatures of over 4,000 voters were
secured, calling for a special election. But before this was resorted to, the League persuaded
the Council to adopt an ordinance compelling
the use of proper fenders and the reduction of
the speed to four miles an hour within the
heart of the city, and to eight miles an hour
farther out. Since the adoption of this ordinance, several persons whom the cars have
struck and who would undoubtedly have been
killed under the former existing conditions,
have been safely carried by the fenders until the

motorman was able to bring his car to a stand-
still. If nothing further is accomplished by
this League, it has amply justified its existence
by this bit of legislation so essential to the public welfare.

A recent organization is that of the City
Club, which has for its purpose the consideration and discussion of municipal topics. It
has a membership of over 250, and gath-
ers once a week at the lunch hour. There
are no other obligations connected with this
club than the occasional attendance. While
it is not the intention of this organization to
take up active work, its discussions are of
great benefit, clarifying the minds of its members on important issues and as all the public officials are invited to its meetings, it will
serve as a means of linking together the administration and those interested in best development of the city.

The Civic League is an organization of young
men, formed for the purpose of study along
civic lines. Meeting at regular periods, it
has subjects of local interest presented for consideration. Thus acquainting themselves in-
timately with local conditions, these young
men are fitting themselves to play a strong
part in the affairs of the future.

In their proper place, we wish to refer to the
great work for civic betterment undertaken
by organized women; by the temperance
forces; by the Federated Churches; by the

social settlements; labor unions; by musical clubs and art centers; and by large-hearted individuals. No matter how large this city may become, because of this grand band of earnest workers which will grow rather than diminish, slums will never exist, public ownership will become an established fact, thus protecting the city official from the bribery of public utility corporations. Thus many of the evils which have afflicted us will trouble us no more, and instead, new visions of a larger brotherhood will fill the hearts of all.

But all the work for civic betterment is not being done as the result of private initiative. The city itself is seeking the moral uplift, physical improvement, and enjoyment of all the people. As we have seen, the work for the City Beautiful is also work for the civic betterment. The Park Board with all its plans for breathing spots and nature resorts, the Municipal Art Commission, and the Playground Commission, are all to be included in the list of those forces working for civic betterment.

No city has ever been made permanently better that has not given serious attention to its delinquents. A constant stream of wrecked and ruined humanity pours through the police courts and jails. It is necessary for us to inquire into the underlying causes of this condition. A Los Angeles writer puts it thus tersely: "The civilized world is just at the threshold of a deeper and more complete realization of the responsibility of society for the existence of those delinquents and of the price it pays for their existence. The spirit of angry revenge that has existed for so many centuries and the fatalistic sentiment that these conditions are inevitable, and that no one is to blame for them, are in turn giving way to a belief that society is to blame, and that it holds the means of remedy in its own hands. The juvenile courts, the children's playgrounds, factory legislation, compulsory education, better housing conditions, vacation schools, fresh-air movements—these are the things that strike at the root of the trouble, and in the course of one or two generations will make the world materially better. If every child born into the world could be sure of light and air and exercise, cleanliness, sufficient food, education, amusement, and decent surroundings, there would be almost no delinquents; and if the few that came into existence in spite of such a regime were justly and kindly but firmly dealt with, there would be hope for their reformation. These things are not impossible; they are merely deferred."

But society must care not alone for the delinquents, but also for the dependents and the defectives. The back door thrust and the wayside dole will never furnish any satisfactory relief. In Los Angeles there is not a great amount of poverty, if we accept the definition of Robert Hunter, who maintains that "those who are in poverty may be able to get a bare sustenance, but they are not able to obtain those necessaries which will enable them to maintain a state of physical efficiency." When we consider that there are no less than ten million persons in the United States who are underfed, underclothed and poorly housed, Los Angeles will be found to fall far below the average in her proportion of dependents.

For many years, owing to the rapid development of the city, a large proportion of the laboring men of the city have been able to secure work at not less than $2.00 a day, and men with trades have been able to secure even as much as $6.00 a day. There being no time lost in winter, and no demand for extra clothing and coal, there are few reasons why anyone should fall below the line of physical efficiency. Yet there are always some who are not able to make even a limited success of life. There are incompetents and defectives who need parental care. Temporary sickness or accidents; chronic disease, desertion, strikes and lockouts; the result of economic conditions beyond their control; drinking or gambling—any of these may send families below the line of self-support, where they may need help. It is the testimony of all social workers that the average working men will seek charity only after every other resort has failed. That being so, the condition in New York City must be very bad, since we read that one in every ten who died there was buried in the Potter's Field. In Los Angeles it is rare that a member of a working man's family ever receives such a burial. For those who are bread winners, the most effective charity is that which helps men to help themselves, finding them employment, or as in New Zealand, sending them where there is a scarcity of labor. The Associated Charities of Los Angeles is a well-organized institution, whose offers of assistance are based on investigation and actual knowledge, and are accompanied by the touch of personal sympathy. Mr. A. J. Pillsbury, Secretary of the State Board of Examiners, speaking of Los Angeles, says: "When a case of distress is reported to the Associated Charities, the first thing they do is to relieve such pressing need as may exist. Then they investigate the causes and remove them if possible. It may be lack of work, or it may be a husband who has run away. In the first case, work is found; and in the second, the husband is found if possible, and straightway coerced into the path of forsaken duty. In short, they try to do whatever is necessary under the infinitely varying circumstances of human distress. It may be a widow who could do fairly well but for the incessant demands of young children, and then perhaps relatives can be persuaded to come forward, or it may be that some charitable family will make itself responsible for

A TYPICAL WORKING MAN'S HOME

one of the children until the sun shines out
again from behind the clouds. Think how infinitely better this is than an immediate appeal
for the State funds and the State machinery,
a pauperization inflicted when there is not need
for it; a loss of human dignity instead of the
increase of human dignity that comes from an
unobtrusive and sympathetic helping hand.
Think of the saving of the public funds, and
think, too, of the number of children who are
thus guarded from the delinquency and criminality that must surely follow upon neglect
for which the overworked and harassed
mother can hardly be held responsible."

The real success of organized charity lies not
in detecting so many frauds, or in placing so
many persons in institutions, or in relieving
immediate want. This does not go far enough
if the inspirational side of charity is left out.
The friendly visitor by advice or because of
large knowledge is able to encourage and
gradually bring back to self-support and to
self-respect the one who had dropped below
the line. Statistics and reports necessary as
they may be to scientific charity, must be supplemented by the human touch. Palliative
measures are not sufficient. Poverty and vice
and crime are sicknesses of society and can be
cured as readily as bad diseases, but the cause
of the disease must first of all be discovered
if a permanent cure is to be effected.

The present industrial system produces
5

much of the poverty that confronts us; it results in accidents that cripple the bread winner, perhaps for life; the breaking up of the unity of the family, because both parents and children are forced to the factories and workshops, under unwholesome sanitary conditions. "The hoe-man in the making," Edwin Markham calls the child worker. When society remedies these and other evils, we will be well on the way to the cure of poverty. The most difficult and delicate charity question in this city is the care of the vagrants who drift here for the winter, and the helplessly sick who are sent here to be cured by the climate, and who often come with the expectation that they will be cared for by the philanthropic societies while in our midst.

In the belief that cleanliness of person is not only elevating in its effect upon mind and morals, but also necessary to the health and to the warding off of disease, many cities have in the last fifteen years undertaken the erection of Municipal Bath Houses. While in Europe such bath and wash houses have existed for many years, and while in America there were some private enterprises and a few Municipal Beach and Floating Baths, it remained for one man to work, almost single handed, for the universal adoption of public baths. Dr. Simon Baruch of New York was the first promoter of the movement, and but for him, there might not be a free public bath in the United States today. He based his plea on the fact that in cleanliness lies the essential principle of sanitation. He pointed out the absurdity of the annual expenditure of millions to relieve distress, when almost nothing was done to prevent disease and improve the condition of the poor while still in health. When in Los Angeles several months ago, Dr. Baruch urged the city to be up-to-date and introduce the rain bath, now so common in Eastern cities. In a newspaper interview, he said: "I confess that I have done more to save life and prevent the spread of disease in my work for public baths than in all my work as a physician. It is the duty of the municipality to prevent disease. It is the duty of the municipality to prevent immorality. I believe that money spent for public baths where people can go and get clean does more toward raising the standard of health and morality than a much greater amount spent in any other way." To this New York's Health Commissioner adds that public baths tend to lessen pneumonia and tuberculosis, the chief cause of mortality among New York's poor, because bathing reduces the liability to colds and throat trouble. The Boston Bath Commission reports "a marked decrease in juvenile arrests during the past ten years and that the work of the Bath Department has been the greatest single agency affecting this vital improvement in public morals."

The first baths to be opened all the year around were in Yonkers and Chicago; then followed Boston, Baltimore, Albany, Cleveland, and tardily, New York. Once started, this latter city is rapidly building baths in all parts, and if the present plans are carried out, it will soon have a system of free baths, the like of which has not been known since the passing of the noted baths of ancient Rome. The Philadelphia system has become so popular that in a single week during last summer more than half a million men, women and children sought relief from the sweltering heat within these free bath houses.

The cost of buildings in the various cities differs greatly, some cities preferring marble and slate and fancy fixtures, others being content with open beams and with unplastered brick. Dover Street Baths in Boston cost $870,000 for forty sprays; Rivington Baths in New York cost but $104,000 for sixty-seven sprays. In Chicago the cost varies from $7,500 to $15,000 for from fifteen to thirty-five sprays. Baltimore has been able to provide houses with thirty to forty-five sprays at a cost of from $25,000 to $40,000. Dr. Baruch considers the expenditure of the higher amount as wanton extravagance. The kind of bath to be used was a vexed question in the early days of bath house building. The principles of sanitation, thorough cleansing, together with economy of space, time, water and service

all had to be taken into consideration. The
solution of this problem led to the abolition
of the tub and the adoption of the German
rain, or shower bath. In this way the expense of the tub was avoided; there was a saving of time required both for the filling of the
tub and the scrubbing of it after the bath;
furthermore, the danger of contagion was reduced to a minimum. The time required for
a shower bath is much less than that required
for a tub bath, for the force of the water aids
in the removal of all accumulated matter; besides this, no soiled water touches the body.
Because of these things, a shower bath is more
refreshing and cleansing.

In Los Angeles there has been no movement toward the establishment of Municipal
Baths, the principal reason being the lack of
water, but with the coming of the supply from
Owens River, drinking fountains, shower
baths, and swimming pools will no doubt be
established in every part of the city. Even now
in the Eighth Ward artesian wells produce a
fine quality of sulphur water which could be
utilized and made healthful as well as cleansing.
An extensive private-owned bath house in the
western part of the city is thus supplied with
health-giving water. The Y. M. C. A. furnishes a swimming pool, tubs and showers
in their temporary quarters, and will have more
extensive accommodations in their new building. The only public bath in the city was

established five years ago by the Bethlehem
Institutional Church at the corner of Vignes
and Ducommun Streets. This was made
possible by the gift of a prominent philanthropist. The building contains a plunge,
thirty by sixty feet, three tubs for women,
four tubs for men, and two showers. The
charge is nominal—five cents for soap and
towel, or for trunks and towel to those who
use the plunge. No one is turned away for
lack of money. About half of the cities having baths, make no charge whatever, the baths
being as free as the parks. This seems to be
the ideal plan wherever possible. An average
of 30,000 baths are given in the Bethlehem
Baths each year. This institution has just
completed a new bath house at Railroad and
N. Main Streets. This has four tubs for men,
four for women, and twelve shower baths.
There are 2,500 men working in the factories
and foundries within three minutes' walk of
this place, and as there have never been public
bathing facilities in that part of the city, it will
prove a great boon to those toil-begrimed men.

A comparatively new movement is the introduction of baths into public school houses.
Boston, New York and many other cities have
adopted the school bath, reporting a marked
improvement in the general health of the children and a resultant alertness as well. The
city of Gottingen, Hanover, Germany, was the
first to introduce the school bath, and Tolman's

report on public baths gives the method in use, and the results: "The baths were ready for use in 1885. No compulsion was used, and at first only a few children went down, but after two months, about seventy-five per cent took part in the bathing. Each scholar who wishes, receives a bath once a fortnight, on one of the four full days when school is open. The class which bathes studies some lesson which does not require the presence of the whole class. From six to nine children, according to size, go down at once, and when they have had time to undress, a second set are sent down. The first step under the douches, two or three under each douche, and when they have bathed, the others are ready to take their places. Thus the douches are kept in use, and the time occupied is comparatively small—a class of fifty-one boys bathing in fifty minutes. Girls and younger children take a considerably longer time. The disturbance of lessons is not so great as was feared. Only a few children are absent at any one time, and these can be easily controlled—the boys by the janitor, and the girls by the janitress.

"A towel is brought by each bather, whilst bathing caps and petticoats are supplied to the larger girls. Precaution is taken to avoid cold immediately after bathing. The children go back to warmed classrooms and cool off gradually, no bathing being allowed within half an hour before school closes.

" 'The quickness and willingness to learn after bathing; the education of the sense of cleanliness; the futherance of the health of the children, are such important and real results of this arrangement,' says School Director Personn, 'that I cannot but express to the city the wish that, if possible, similar bathing establishments might be introduced into other public schools.'

"Already it has been found that parents send cleaner and tidier children to the handsome new school buildings; now their pride makes them anxious that neither the janitress nor their fellow scholars should see their ragged or dirty underclothing. There are few families so lost to better feelings that this has no effect upon them, and in those where drink has driven the sense of honor away, charity must give clothes to the poor children."

In this city three years ago, the principal of the Amelia Street School secured permission, after some opposition, to place a tub in one of the out-buildings. This has been used in a similar manner to those baths just described. There are so many children not having bathing facilities in their home, that this has been well patronized from the beginning, and it is regarded by the School Board as a successful innovation. Two other schools have established baths—the Utah Street and the Castellar Street Schools, both of which are in the foreign districts.

Another movement for civic betterment

THE BETHLEHEM BATHS

which has not yet been recognized as a necessity in this city is the establishment of Public Comfort Stations, giving The Public, use of lavatories, urinals and toilets. The existing coffee clubs furnish such accommodations; the hotels give them to those who are as well dressed as their patrons, and many stores have special retiring rooms for women; but otherwise the saloons offer the only conveniences for the average man of the street. The patronage of the saloon is increased greatly in return for the use of these facilities. Most men who use them spend money over the bar, or they meet with other men who treat them, thus forming oftentimes the beginnings of a debauch. Temperance workers might well turn their attention to this movement as an essential factor in the promotion of better morals. On the Continent one meets with these conveniences every five or six blocks; in Paris they are sometimes so noticeable as to offend public decency. Their obtrusiveness is remedied in this country by building them beneath the street, or by constructing them in the shape of artistic chalets at the junctions of streets. In Europe each station has its attendant who keeps everything scrupulously clean. The urinals are always free to the public, and usually one toilet. For the other toilets and for the use of soap and towels for the lavatories, five cents is usually charged.

Well-kept Public Comfort Stations serve as

powerful assistants to the Board of Health—
"Examples of what can be done to render such
structures comfortable and inoffensive, introducing among the lower class habits of self-
respect and cleanliness that will improve the
condition of the crowded quarters."

Four sites naturally suggest themselves for
the location of underground stations. One of
these is at the junction of Spring and Main
Streets, where the drinking fountain is located. Built underground, nicely tiled and
ventilated, it could have above ground an artistic fountain. Such an arrangement would
not interfere with the sewer pipes below the
surface or with the traffic above. This will
be a congested spot when the new post-office is
completed. Another could be placed underground in the little City Hall Park on Broad-
way, and not interfere at all with the plants
or flowers. The third should replace the present
unsatisfactory toilet in the Sixth Street Park,
being built either underground, or as a neatly
shaped chalet, painted in colors harmonious
with the foliage. The south junction of Spring
and Main Streets suggests itself as the site
for the fourth underground station. Certain
cities have erected chalets for ladies, with a
notion store in front, thus making it possible
for ladies to enter without embarrassment, as
the entrance is always through the shops. Los
Angeles ought not to be behind in this world-

wide movement for the comfort and welfare of its citizens.

Housing conditions in Los Angeles are just beginning to receive attention. As the Greater City comes nearer to its realization, the leaders in social thought are more and more determined that it shall be a city of homes, and therefore a city without slums. Instead of the pent-up millions in other cities, that from necessity or choice know only a contracted indoor existence, here will be found only healthy, happy families, scattered over a vast area; twenty-five persons to the acre, rather than 1,000 as in the tenement districts of our large cities. No one who is familiar with even the model tenement will ever desire to see it established in this city. New York with its sea-girt land, vast population, and lack of rapid transit, must needs live high up in the air, in dark contracted rooms, with scarcity of light and sunshine; but Los Angeles, with its vast stretches of hill and valley, of plain and seashore, every acre of which would furnish a homesite unequaled elsewhere, offers freer and happier conditions.

There are no slums in Los Angeles in the sense that a slum is a vicious congested district, for one must always distinguish between districts filled with working men and their families, and those filled with vicious immoral characters. There are slum people in Los Angeles, but no one district where they are centered. For the most part the poor live in single cottages, with dividing fences and flowers in the front yard, and oftentimes with vegetables in the back yard. Even in the most congested districts children can be kept within the yard, if so desired. Homes for the people; pure hearts for pure hearth stones, are the mottoes for a city like this.

Sonoratown, as the old pueblo is called, has still a remnant of its original Mexican dwellers in adobe houses, crowded by the incoming Italians, Slavonians and Syrians. For these newcomers, one-story shacks were built in the rear of the old Mexican houses. As might be expected, these courts, as they were called, soon became as vicious as the tenement conditions in Eastern cities, save that here fresh air and out-door life could be had the year around. The new housing ordinance has compelled the landlords owning these courts to bring them up to a higher degree of sanitary efficiency.

The coming of the Russians in large numbers to this city caused for a time much unhealthy crowding, with several families in houses intended for only one family, but these people are industrious and thrifty, and are now buying houses of their own.

The worst congestion that existed in the city was found on Utah Street, just east of the river, where those Mexicans lived who were brought in from Mexico to work on the trolley lines. The land in that locality was divided into tiny lots which were rented for one or two dollars a month. On each of these lots was built a shack of hammered-out cans, old boxes, or burlap, with no yard space nor sanitary appliances of any sort. The toilets were of earth, and were used in common. In order to study this condition, a Housing Commission was appointed by the Mayor, composed of prominent social workers, which succeeded in having the City Council pass the ordinance just referred to. Defining a house court as a parcel or area of land on which are grouped houses or habitations, used or designed for the occupancy of families, and upon which parcel or area, the vacant or unoccupied property thereof, surrounding or abutting, is intended for common use by the inhabitants thereof, the ordinance demands that at least thirty per cent of the house court shall remain unoccupied. Houses must be made of substantial building material, suitable for permanent construction; earth floors are not permitted; there must be a space of seven feet between the floor and the ceiling; and there must be windows for ventilation, equal to ten per cent of floor space. Separate toilet facilities must be maintained for men and women, with no less than one toilet for every ten persons. Hydrants must be provided with hoppers and drains, and no less than one for every three persons in court. The surface and open spaces in the court must be covered with sand, or gravel, or asphaltum. In several instances the landlords, rather than submit to the expense of renovating the houses and repairing the courts, have evicted their tenants. This is especially true on Utah Street, where nearly all the courts were cleaned out.

Meanwhile the laying out of new subdivisions far out beyond the city limits, makes cheap and desirable home sites, obtainable for a multitude of working men, where they are able to build cheap bungalows or California houses, or at least to erect tents. "The Family Unit," the desire of the sociologist, can be recovered, when by rapid transit, giving a fare of from five to seven cents for a thirty minutes' ride, the working man can be induced to locate with his family far from the noisy city. No work for civic betterment is worth more than this.

In this Beautiful and Better City that is to be, the men of wealth will do much toward bringing about the desired results. It is a question in these days, how much a man's wealth is really private wealth. Did the owner create it? Is it the result of his brain power or the work of his hands alone? Wealth is social, and ought to be thought of more as common wealth. And as men come to realize this, they will gladly give more and more to the common good. Parks and playgrounds will be donated; fountains and monuments built;

music halls established; settlement houses erected; schools and colleges endowed; institutions of all kinds will be planned for the people's health and enjoyment. It is a hopeful sign that in the present day, as never before, church and social workers, Captains of Industry and Knights of Labor, are all interested in the building of the Better City.

CHAPTER IV.

SOCIAL CENTERS

The modern city has many customs as well as costumes brought into it from lands across the sea. For want of a common language and of common ideals of government, the New England town meeting could not now be made the social and political center which it was of old. Nor can the Church be the unifying force which it was in the day of the old white meeting house on the green, for in the modern un-American city, the Church is divisive rather than unitive. A common religion has not yet been found for the Roman and Greek Church; for Jew, Armenian, Buddhists, Confucianists, Mohammedans, and the innumerable sects of a divided Protestantism. They are all God's children; yet the problem is to teach them to live and walk together as brethren. This is indeed a new world. In old Jerusalem, the people live today as in the time of Christ. In the new Jerusalem which is to arise in our midst, the original type of Hebrew, Slav, Teuton, Scandinavian, Briton, Latin, and Asiatic, will be lost and in their places will be the American. A new type in language, dress, social intelligence and spiritual ideals will develop. The world at large is waiting the evo-

OUR RUSSIAN NEIGHBORS FROM THE TRANS-CAUCASUS

lution of the American, with the conviction
that when he is developed, he will be the
noblest work of God. But no man can sit
idly by and watch the making of the American, for he feels that he himself is a factor, and
therefore a part of the process. A new occupation is open to those whose hearts are
stirred by the calls of humanity and by the
thought of a larger brotherhood. To join with
others in the effort to bring together the divided units of a cosmopolitan city, is an effort
large enough for any man.

Each city has its own foreign problem to
deal with, one nationality usually predominating. The story of the effort to make Los Angeles an American city and a better city should
be of interest to social workers in other localities.

Long before the American flag floated over
the hilltop above this pueblo, this section was
peopled by those from afar, whose tongue was
musical and whose attire was picturesque.
Their descendants today are proud to be
known as the real Californians. Oftentimes
poor because robbed of their lands, they have
either been absorbed by the new life, or remain
proud of name and title—a reminder of the
early days of Alta California. Do not make
the mistake of calling them Mexicans; rather
call them Spanish or Californians. Not until
recent years has there been an influx of Mexicans from our sister republic on the south.

6

With the trolley building came the need for cheap labor and the bringing in of hundreds of laborers with their families. These Mexicans being very poor and accustomed to a bare life in their own land, have chosen to live in shacks closely crowded together, thus forming the city's first housing problem. With the exception of the quick use of the knife after drinking cheap wine, they are a peaceable, hardworking people, some saving their money and going back to Mexico with what seems to them to be a small fortune. Many of the young men and women have entered into the night schools of the different social centers and are becoming educated and refined. By nature musical, they have formed bands and orchestras. Among them, and especially among the Californians, are talented singers, who at social gatherings, delight the people with "La Paloma" and other beautiful Spanish songs. Some of the leaders of the Californians are reviving the old-time Spanish dances, thus adding much to popular entertainments. In fact, Los Angeles, with its Spanish life left out, would lose much of its charm. While the Church and settlement are aiding much in the development of these laborers, the greatest transforming power at work upon them is as with all other foreigners, the public school. This is the real social center—a common meeting ground for the races, giving inspiration and aspiration to thousands. Go into the schoolrooms in Los Angeles set aside for non-English speaking children and watch the gradual change in dress, in step, in eye and voice. Receiving daily higher ethical standards, they become little missionaries for good in their own home. Three of the city schools are largely filled with foreigners, or rather with future Americans.

Along with the Mexicans came the people of sunny Italy. Beside common laborers, large numbers of these people have entered into the business life of the city and have become very successful. While speaking of themselves as the "Italian Colony," they are living more and more in scattered homes throughout the city, and are quickly becoming Americanized. This is also the way in which the very industrious Germans and Scandinavians are becoming an integral part of the city. Many Jewish people are prominent in commercial lines, and are leaders in ethical movements for the good of the city. There are no Hebrews in extreme poverty. With a little start, every newcomer is able to support himself in some small business without falling beneath the line of self-support into pauperism. The Slavonians are hard workers with pick and shovel, and show a capacity for receiving American ideas, learning a little business and a little English, but always reminding one of the Old World.

Five years ago there came a young Russian

from the Trans-Caucasus to Russian friends in
Canada. Drifting down to Los Angeles, he
was so delighted with the country that he
wrote back to his people to come thither at
once. They belonged to a religious sect known
as the "Brotherhood of Spiritual Christians."
They were sober, industrious "mujiks" or
farmers, yet persecuted as only Russia knows
how to persecute her political and religious
dissenters. Like Tolstoi, these men were non-
resistants. When the Czar ordered them to
fight the Japanese, they refused, and to escape
the punishment which would have been theirs
as a penalty for their refusal, they began to
steal out of Russia, and to start on their long
journey overland through Germany and across
the waters, carrying with them their beloved
"samovar" and a big bundle of clothes. Many
hundreds of these people have come to this
city, hoping to obtain land, and to bring over
the entire 25,000 belonging to their brotherhood. Two attempts at colonizing have been
made—one in Hawaii and one in Lower California, but both have proved partial failures.
Having secured work in the lumber yards and
in factories at good wages, the majority will
become a part of the city life and forget that
they ever were foreigners. All of the young
men have adopted American clothes, and some
of the older ones also, except on Sunday, when
they go to their meeting clothed in the Russian
peasant's garb. The women are slow to

change, and with their elaborately embroidered, many-colored gowns, look very picturesque as they walk in groups to their Sunday service. Through the influence of the Bethlehem Night Schools, many of the young men are quite Americanized, and they declare that they are "no longer Paruski, but Americanski." As the years go by, these men will become the political leaders of their brethren.

Many Greek young men also have come to this city from Athens, and have entered into business. Being separated from their families at first, as soon as they make sufficient money, they send for their relatives in Greece, and thus the colony is growing constantly larger and more permanent.

No tourist ever leaves the city without a visit to Chinatown. A few years ago there were many thousand Celestials packed away in their narrow quarters, but owing to the strict enforcement of the Exclusion Law, there has in recent years been a steady decrease in numbers, up to the time when the Chinatown in San Francisco was wiped out, and many of its inhabitants joined the stream of refugees who came hither to start their life anew. Several church missions have labored among these people, faithfully Christianizing them, and helping them to better living. Without thought or chance of becoming Americans, they have unconsciously prepared themselves as leaders for the new China across the sea, in the day of her fast approaching awakening. While many of the children are in the public schools and are rapidly becoming Americanized, they also receive training in a Chinese school, taught by a teacher brought direct from Canton. A few of the second generation, whose parents were taught in the California schools and who are themselves registered voters, look and act so much like Americans that it is easy to believe that if the Chinese had come with the intention of staying in this country, they might easily have added their part to the citizenship of this great nation.

During the summer months, there is a Japanese population in this city of 3,000, while in winter there are over 5,000. At the celebration of the Emperor's birthday, several thousand joined in the shout of "Banzai"—"May he live a thousand years." In this large crowd there was not to be seen a single Japanese garment worn by either man or woman. The Japanese are always well dressed, cleanly and orderly. Many work in families that they may have the opportunity of attending the public or night schools. Unlike the Chinese, they do not live close together in colonies, but scatter about the city in boarding houses kept by their own people. There are several missions and churches among them, and one Buddhist temple. A few are engaged in banking and commercial enterprises, but the majority work in ordinary labor on the ranches and on the railroad. Recently many have brought their families to this country, buying land and settling down as though they intended to remain for life. The Association of Japanese Christians is a strong factor in the moral and ethical development of these young men so far away from home and exposed to temptations on every hand.

Because there is no serious housing problem and little grinding poverty, social workers can devote more time to the real things that make for the larger life. There are four centers of life that need developing: The family center, the social center, the school center, and the ethical or spiritual center. Of this last, we wish to treat more fully in another chapter, an inspirational center being absolutely necessary for the full rounded life of any community. Without direct ethical or spiritual teaching, many of our modern methods may have no more permanent uplift than did the baths or the games of Rome, or the debates on the Acropolis of Athens.

Social and religious workers have always maintained that the development of the family center is the most important. Grant perfect family life and the majority of the philanthropic and reformatory institutions would close their doors. To the end of perfecting family life, a multitude of agencies are always at work—the Church, the School, the Court, the Settlement, Organized Charity, Municipal, County and State Boards, as well as Philanthropic Societies. Owing to the influx of foreigners with low ideals of family life, the problem in the crowded tenements is made exceedingly difficult. Yet in all the cities there is a noticeable improvement in the home life of the people. The social center has in the last score of years become a great factor in the betterment of the conditions under which men live. Because of the rapid growth of cities in the last half century, resulting from the development of industrialism and the importation of alien workers, there has developed a condition of slum life which is so interwoven with political corruption that the Church and organized charity hardly knows how to cope with it. They see the sorrow, the suffering and the sin, and try to rescue the individual, but they do not fully understand the causes which are making for social corruption, and which result in the degeneration of whole neighborhoods.

The great Apostle of Social Study and Social Help—the John the Baptist of all new social movements—was Arnold Toynbee, a young Oxford man, who, stirred by a passion for the better social order, took up a residence in the midst of the terrible degradation of Whitechapel. A student of conditions, a sympathetic friend, he lived the loving life in the midst of the unlovely. In a few short years he wore himself out in the service of mankind, yet the world has been made richer

THE SETTLEMENT HOUSE

by far, by that short life, than it ever has been by any Captain of Industry who has merely amassed a fortune. This life gave the initial impulse to the modern movement of the social settlements. The great Toynbee Hall in Whitechapel is its fitting memorial, together with the ever-increasing number of settlements in the hearts of the cities of the world.

Actuated by the same noble purpose that stirred the heart of Toynbee, many of the world's choicest scholars, and large-hearted men and women, have chosen to live where they saw the greatest need, thus forming social centers for the "unification of neighborhood life, laboratory work for the study and analysis of social and industrial problems, and as a common meeting place for mutual interpretation of widely differing ideals, economic conditions and standards of living."

A universal definition of the Social Settlement has never been formulated. Everett P. Wheeler gives as its fundamental idea, the following: "It is a home in an industrial center, where employer and employed, educated and uneducated, rich and poor, can meet on friendly terms; come to an understanding of the human element that vitalizes them all, and so remove the narrow prejudice that ignorance begets and that keeps men asunder. The Settlement has for its fundamental basis the Fatherhood of God and the brotherhood of man. These are eternal." As Dr. Graham

Taylor puts it, "we who at the Chicago Commons share the common lot, choose to live for our own and others' sake, where we seem to be the most needed, rather than where the neighborhood seems to offer the most social privilege or prestige. We are here to be all we can to the people and to receive all they are to us as friends and neighbors. We assume the full obligations and claim all the rights of citizenship in a community with whose interests we identify ourselves, whose conditions we share, and for whose home, happiness, political freedom and progress, we try to do our part."

The settlement workers are not missionaries going down to the people to lift them up, but rather being just "folks," living the simple life of friendship and neighborliness. Their motto is—each for all, and all for each. Grant the spirit of service, and the development is natural. Given the man or woman with the spirit of the Nazarene, and two rooms in a tenement may be a settlement. Nor will it be long until about this center neighbors will meet for self-improvement and mutual benefit. Then a larger building will be found necessary; soon mothers' meetings, making for the betterment of home life, will be held; men's clubs for the creation of better citizens and for the overthrow of boss rule, and the purification of politics will be organized; boys' and girls' clubs will be formed to give an object in life and af-

ford a normal outlet to childhood's energies,
thus breaking the power of the street gang,
and making a rallying center for all that up-
lifts and refines. The effect upon the immediate neighborhood will be far reaching, yet
even greater will be the reflex influence upon
the educated and the well-to-do classes in the
community. It will result in the rousing of
the social conscience, the breaking down of
social barriers; it will also give an enlarged
idea of life and of social service; and will furnish an opportunity for men of leisure to devote time and money to the social uplifting of
the community life.

In Los Angeles a movement of this kind was
started thirteen years ago by a group of college
women, students of sociology, in the original
city, the old pueblo, for some time in an adobe
house of the old type; finally in a two-story
house containing fourteen rooms, owned by
the Settlement Association, and located at
Castelar and Alpine Streets. The various
nationalities have there a common meeting
place. The Californian, the Mexican, the
Italian, the Syrian, the Slavonian, who constitute the crowded dwellers of the neighborhood,
know they are welcome at this house at any
time. The boys and girls have been reached
through the various clubs and classes; the
mothers, through the sewing clubs and clothing departments; the men through the night
schools and entertainments. This settlement

is unique in having secured the first district nurse appointed by any municipality, and at present it has charge of three nurses, under the pay of the city. They are devoting their entire time, not alone to the neighborhood, but to the public schools throughout the city, and responding to calls throughout the city. Directing the people how to care for the sick—preventitive treatment—rather than work with cases, is the special function of the District Nurse. She has proven a great help to the Health Department, by giving notice of the first appearance of any virulent disease, thus making it possible to check contagion and to rob the County Hospital of many a patient. The members of this Association are prominent in the work of civic betterment—in securing better housing conditions, in advancing the work of the public schools, in the playground movement, and Juvenile Court. The Association itself is a fountain of good works.

Another settlement is the Brownson House, on Vignes and Jackson Streets, conducted for several years by a number of prominent Catholic young women. On Sunday they hold a morning mass, having an altar in the Assembly Hall, covered at other times by a screen. They also conduct a Sunday School, the usual clubs for boys and girls, hold mothers' meetings, and furnish literary and social entertainments. They have recently opened a day nursery on Vignes Street, near the Brownson

House. Their broad spirit of fellowship and their sense of the larger brotherhood is evidenced by their readiness to coöperate with all who are working for the common good.

The cluster of institutions known as Bethlehem deserves to be called a settlement, for many earnest workers have resided in them for years, in one of the most congested districts in the city, laboring along the usual settlement lines.

Separate groups such as these ought to be multiplied in this growing city, yet it seems to me that the next step should be to utilize as social centers the public school buildings with their grounds, now unused outside of school hours. This movement has made great headway in Eastern cities where the roofs and basements of buildings are being used for public playgrounds; the rooms at night for reading rooms, and study rooms where backward pupils may receive extra help, as night schools for grown-ups, or as halls for popular lectures and entertainments. Belonging to the people, they ought to be used for the public good. It is a good sign to see the people coming, slowly, to possess that which is their own. The use of the school property in summer time for school gardens and summer schools, is certainly good use of invested money. The Los Angeles schools are slowly working toward this ideal. Here and there the borders of yards are planted with flowers and vegetables, and a start has been made in the use of outside plots for garden work. The three vacation playgrounds established by the Playground Commission have been taken over for the school term by the schools themselves. A man teacher in each school keeps the playground open for two hours after school each day, and on Saturday afternoons. For two years one of the schools was kept open in the evenings for a reading room, and once a week lectures and entertainments were held in it for the parents of the children. The neighborhood use of the public school is becoming more and more recognized, and it is being made a social and a recreational as well as an educational center.

Three years ago the Amelia Street School introduced a bath tub, and others have followed. The number of school nurses has been increased and all are more than kept busy. Heads have been cleansed, contagious diseases have been carefully investigated, bruises treated, eyes and ears examined and instruction given in hygiene to the children. When it was found necessary, the help of a good physician has been advised, and the treatment continued at home. Absences because of illness have been at once investigated, and in this way any hidden contagion has been discovered. The school board has established probation, truant and parental schools, with a measure of medical inspection.

Movements for social centers are not confined to settlements or schools. In New York the movement for establishing Neighborhood Social Halls free from the saloon curse and the low dance hall, has resulted in the building of the well-equipped Clinton Hall in the Jewish Quarter. It is to be hoped that many such halls may be established elsewhere, giving clean social life to those who now know only bad environment. Since the opening in Boston of the first municipal gymnasium in 1897, it has been so largely patronized that many more have been built in other parts of the city.

The most unique movement for the establishment of social centers is that of the South Park Commission of Chicago, sometimes called "Chicago's ten-million-dollar experiment in social redemption." This gigantic scheme originated in the dream of one man who thought that there was a greater social need than could be supplied by private initiative. He gained his point after much effort, by having appointed a Board of Commissioners, with power to buy small plots of ground in the congested districts of the South Side, and to set them apart perpetually for the enjoyment of all the people. In the dozen or more parks which have been secured, there are large playfields for almost every kind of game; outdoor gymnasiums for men and women, swings, teeters, children's lawns, sand plots, and a wading pool for the little folks. There are large, enclosed swimming tanks, free to all, indoor gymnasiums, club rooms for women, men, girls and boys; assembly halls which can be used by the people at any time, the only restriction being that no refreshments be brought in— use being made of the refectory below. This movement for large, well-equipped social centers will surely spread to other cities. The first building similar to these, in this city, is soon to be built in the Eighth Ward.

As a result of the social awakening, new professions are coming into existence, as for instance, that of the Sanitary Engineer. His social service lies in the direction of the work of sanitary rehabilitation after great disasters, like that at Galveston or at San Francisco, the elimination of mosquitos and malaria, and the suppression of such epidemics as typhoid. The methods used are those of educating the public in simple methods of protecting themselves against disease, but at the same time he can use autocratically the power vested in health laws, to burn houses, sieze schools for hospitals, and compel the police to see to the enforcement of sanitary regulations.

There is a demand in every city for the appointment of a Superintendent of Social Service—a person of broad education and large heart, who will have the oversight of all municipal social centers; a man free from poli-

THE WOMAN'S CLUB HOUSE

tics, who will conduct a social museum containing charts, pictures, designs, or printed matter, all of the world's up-to-date social plans, with an exhibit of all unsanitary or debasing conditions in the city. Such an effort would be a great aid to all city officials in their effort to do their best for their constituents. Los Angeles is having its social awakening. May it take its place in the vanguard of progress, adopting the most approved agencies, that it may speedily become the Better City.

CHAPTER V.

WOMEN'S WORK

The hand that rocks the cradle rules the world. Mother is not only a word of sweet sound, arousing pleasant memories; it stands for the creator of a harmonious household, from which radiates blessed influences. In early times the home was the training school for the moral, mental and physical development of the child. Household duties furnished manual training; the farm or the forest furnished the playground; the social life of the small communities seldom stretched beyond the home. Nearly all the food and clothing was provided by the house-mother. The school taught only the three "R's." In a word, the home was the social unit in which the entire community life was largely expressed.

Industrial life has changed all this arcadian simplicity, with the result that in the great centers of population we have great congestion, people being crowded closely together in flats, in tenement houses and in cottages. Prepared foods and canned goods have made much cooking unnecessary. There are no chores for the children to do and the playground is the street. Clothing is ready made, and the laundry has banished the wash tub.

Adapting itself to changed conditions, the school is reaching out after the child and doing for it much of the work of care taking that was once done by the mother. The Day Nursery and Kindergarten give the child its start. The manual training, cooking and sewing schools, school gardens, and vacation schools, take the child in hand and help him to apply book knowledge to practical life. The dentist, physician, and school nurse look after his physical well-being. The school yards and the school buildings furnish his playground, and these privileges he is coming to share with the entire community. A recent educational magazine prophesies in a recent issue as follows: "In the future the regular public school will probably take the child from morning until the latter part of the afternoon. Noon meals will be served, and the study periods will be interspersed with work and play appropriate to the grade and age of the child. The school will become a workshop and a playground, as well as a place for study and reading books."

The house-mother of the present day relieved from many of the cares of former times is now interested in many things outside of home and church. Influenced by the broader education of her day, she is turning her attention to national, state, municipal and educational affairs. She is asking, and in some states receiving, the ballot; and in civic matters she has already become a power to be reckoned with. Whatever touches the health or morals of the community is of interest to her because she is a woman. As she knows how to make the home a place of beauty, so she is naturally interested in abating nuisances and promoting everything that tends to the development of purity of life in the city at large. With more of patience and persistence than man, she continues in her efforts to reform conditions until results are accomplished. The emancipation of the American woman can best be realized by a study of existing conditions in lands where the harem holds sway or where child widows are numbered by thousands. Under these conditions women live narrow, contracted lives, without social or educational opportunities, and without any far-reaching influence. The women of this and other favored lands, set free from such a narrow environment, are introduced into the larger life of service, and busy themselves in making for the good of their neighborhood, and for the city at large. Manifesting as they often do a greater measure of self-sacrifice than the men of the community, they are entitled to the highest praise.

A study of the modern Woman's Club is of great importance, since it furnishes to women the opportunity for the expression of her highest altruistic impulses. In the beginning of the new social movement, women were as-

sociated together for the acquiring of knowledge pleasantly, and at a far-off range. Today
they are studying unpleasant facts, looking at
them straight in the face and by their combined efforts are seeking to right what is
wrong. As some one has said, "Club wives
and mothers are not satisfied that their children are well nourished and well educated;
they have become members of the race where
once they were members of the family; their
minds and hearts are awake to the needs of
the children of other mothers." The Woman's
Club is a place where the college woman can
take a post-graduate course in civics; a place
for the cultivation of "matriotism" as one has
called it—a term which includes all that is
pure and true and beautiful in thought and life.

In the city of Los Angeles, in her beautiful
home, "El Nido," lives Madame Severance,
"The Mother of Clubs." Her home, surrounded by stately trees and brightest flowers,
is the meeting place of rare souls who come
thither for communion with a great soul, and
for inspiration and uplift. Madame Severance
was the founder of the first woman's club in
our land, known as the New England
Woman's Club of Boston, which was established in 1868. Moving to Los Angeles, she
organized and became the first president of
the original club of this city; and later, in
1891, when the Friday Morning Club was
formed, she was elected as its first leader.

Hers has been an eventful life in the larger fellowship of women. What she has said of another may be fittingly applied to her: "She has always adorned womanhood and worn the white flower of a blameless life in public and in private."

The growth of the club idea has been so rapid, in the opening of the new century, that without careful study it is difficult to understand the scope and the work of the many clubs which seem to overlap one another. A survey of these clubs may be helpful. The Federation of Women's Clubs is divided into the National, State and District Federations. The California Federation consists of six districts: the Northern, San Francisco, Alameda, San Joaquin Valley, Los Angeles, and Southern Districts, which together have many thousand women enrolled. The Los Angeles District has fifty-four clubs, of which twenty-three are located in this city. Many of the larger clubs have a membership of from 100 to 1,000 women. Outside of this Federation, but coöperating with it, are many other groups of women workers, toiling for the world's betterment. Child study circles are found in all the public schools as units in the larger organization, known as the National Congress of Mothers. The National Sunshine Society has its local branches whose aim is to let sunshine into darkened lives. The Women's Parliament, meeting twice a year, has a membership composed of women who are members of some one of the federated clubs. The Needle Work Guild of America has a flourishing branch, whose members contribute each year new garments, which are distributed after careful investigation among the many institutions of the city. Separated from these are the White Ribboners, who in the city, district, state, national and international organizations constitute the great body of the W. C. T. U. Young ladies are working effectively in city and college in the Y. W. C. A., which is worldwide in its organization. In the Assistant's League; the Woman's Exchange; the Grand Army Relief Corps; the Catholic Sisterhoods; the Deaconess' Work; in Social Settlements and on City Commissions; in lodges, Church Societies and Rescue Missions, a multitude of large-hearted women of this city are not only receiving knowledge and inspiration, but are giving of their best to others less fortunate than they. They are interested as one of their number has said "in everything which makes life more beautiful, duty more alluring, and men, women and children happier in each other."

Valuable as is the work of the Women's Clubs, there are still to be found those who speak lightly of this new force. A Washington Senator has been quoted as saying that "this is rapidly becoming a government of the women, for women's views, and by the

Women's Clubs. It is strange that the men do the work of electing us to these positions while women assume the duty of telling us afterwards what they want us to do. The right to petition is apparently more prized than the right of suffrage, and the women do the petitioning."

While each of the clubs in the city is doing a distinct work, there is among them a growing desire to pass on their best for the help of others. The first and largest combination of women in the city is the Friday Morning Club. It is also the broadest in its scope and most inclusive in its fellowship. Its by-laws declare that "all women of Los Angeles and vicinity shall be eligible to membership." Among its thousand members are wage earners and women of the leisure class, those who are leaders in society, and those who devote their entire life to charity and reform. Membership involves no social obligation beyond meeting within the club room parlors. Cliques, professional circles and caste lines are forgotten for the hour, and the spirit of good fellowship prevails. "The discussion of topics of general interest" is given as the object of the club, and this gives broad scope to the programs. Those who are doing something worth doing in the world's work are those who are sought to lead the discussions. There is no obligation to study, but this method of teaching by experts in live, up-to-

THE EBELL CLUB HOUSE

date movements, gives to this club a vitalizing force, which expresses itself in countless activities for the world's good. The rapid growth of the club makes a larger building necessary, and already plans are drawn for a grand and stately structure. The members are loath to leave their beautiful club house on Figueroa Street, which is a perfect adaptation to the mission style, as can be seen from the illustration. A great future is before this club, and there can be no doubt that much that will go to make this a better city will find its inception within the walls of this vine-covered building, or the new home that is to be builded for the women of the next decade.

The Ebell Club, which has nearly 800 members, was organized in 1894 as a study club, modeled after the plan proposed by Dr. Adrian Ebell. Its section work is most interesting. The entire club is divided for the purpose of intensive study, into the following sections: Home, Education, Music, Civics and Art; each under a competent leader. A handsome new club house on Figueroa Street is the home of this band of cultured and earnest women. While seeking helpful knowledge on all subjects pertaining to the home and higher culture of life, their motto might well be "Ich Dien," as they give themselves like their sisters in other clubs, to the moral and spiritual uplift of the entire community.

Much work affecting the welfare of this

municipality is planned and carried to completion by the Civic Association of Los Angeles, which was formed seven years ago, and has at present a membership of 150. The sections into which the Association is divided are as follows: "Outdoor Art, Juvenile Court, Consumer's League, Child Study Circle, Domestic Science, Board of Education, Manual Training, School Lunches, School Decoration, Circulating Art Cabinet, and Lectures. Deeply interested in the welfare of the children, the members of this Association were the first to make a strong plea for playgrounds. They were successful in securing the coöperation of the city in this matter and the appointment of a playground commission, with two members appointed from the Civic Association. Under the leadership of these two women members, the Commission bought a block of land on Violet street and equipped an excellent playground which is largely patronized and is doing the preventitive work which is so much better than reform work. A second playground has been opened in Echo Park. The Playground Commission asked permission to erect playground apparatus in three schoolyards, in the congested districts. This was granted and during the summer vacations these were conducted with such success that when schools opened, the School Board took the responsibility of their care during the entire school year. Compared with other years,

only a very few boys were arrested in the
neighborhood of the playgrounds during the
past year, a record which shows their value
and furnishes an argument for their establishment in other parts of the city. Plans have
been formed for a great recreation center in
the Eighth Ward, similar to those opened by
the South Park Commission in Chicago. The
sites for nine distinct playgrounds have been
selected by the Commission.

Besides showing interest in playgrounds
and in the Juvenile Court the Association is
making war on the smoke nuisance, and is
seeking to have the city make back-door garbage collections. It is also endeavoring to interest the children in bird life. It has like-
wise plans for the establishment of drinking
fountains of a sanitary kind. For the past two
years it has conducted garden contests in three
of the most congested districts. Garden and
flower seeds have been distributed with instructions how to plant and care for the gardens. Certain of the members have visited
each garden many times during the season,
giving advice and encouragement. Not alone
were the homes made beautiful by the flowers,
and food furnished in the vegetables from the
gardens, but the children were given work
which called out their better natures. At the
close of the season, the Mayor and a member
of the Park Commission gave prizes to the
successful contestants, urging them on to even

better work in home decoration during the
coming season. The Association has also
had no small part in carrying out the plans
of the Consumer's League, furnishing a white
list of all stores who treated their help in
a just and humane way. They plead with all
holiday shoppers to buy their holiday goods
early, thus saving the clerks from much overwork due to the later rush. Through this department of the Consumer's League, Owen
Lovejoy, one of the Secretaries of the National
Child Labor Committee, was brought to Los
Angeles, and through his influence the appointment of an inspector of child labor in Southern
California factories seems assured. They are
also interested in the extension of the Park
system and of the flower-lined boulevards
reaching to the sea. Joining with the Church
Federation, they have succeeded in inducing
many of the large stores to close on Saturday
noon during the summer months. The fight
against bill boards and vile posters which has
been begun will be pushed until they are taken
from our streets. This Association was successful in securing the appointment of a tree
warden, who will have general supervision of
tree planting on public streets, inspecting trees
now growing on the streets, and encouraging
with his advice and help the culture of shade
and ornamental trees throughout the city.
Through the work of the women, an annual
Arbor Day celebration has been instituted,

which is becoming a great event among the
school children.

Another far-reaching movement consists of
the Child Study Circles, which are composed of
mothers surrounding every school in the city.
These circles, which include the rich and poor,
the American and the foreign-born women, are
the outgrowth of the National Congress of
Mothers, whose last annual session was held
in this city. The aims and purposes of this
Mother's Congress are set forth as follows:

"To raise the standards of home life. To
develop wiser, better trained parenthood.

"To give young people, ignorant of the
proper care and training of children, opportunities to learn this that they may better perform
the duties of parenthood.

"To bring into closer relation the home and
the school, that parent and teacher may coöperate intelligently in the education of the
child.

"To surround the childhood of the whole
world with that loving wise care in the im-
pressionable years of life, that will develop
good citizens instead of law breakers and
criminals.

"To use systematic effort to this end,
through the formation of Mother's Clubs in
every public school and elsewhere; the establishment of kindergartens and laws which will
adequately care for neglected and dependent
children, in the firm belief that united, con-

certed work for little children will pay better than any other philanthropic work that can be done.

"To carry mother love and mother thought into all that concerns and touches childhood in Home, School, Church, State or Legislation.

"To secure such legislation as will insure that children of tender years may not be tried in ordinary courts, but that each town shall establish juvenile courts and special officers, whose business it shall be to look out for that care which will rescue instead of confirm the child in evil ways.

"To work for such probationary care in individual homes rather than institutions.

"To rouse the whole community to a sense of its duty and responsibility to the blameless, dependent and neglected children because there is no philanthropy which will so speedily reduce the expense of institutions for correction and reform.

"The work of the Congress is civic work in its broadest sense. It is an organized effort for the higher, nobler national life, which can only be attained through the individual homes."

The Ruskin Art Club is not only giving its attention to the study of art, but it has created a Fine Arts Association for the purpose of building a permanent art gallery and museum in this city. It is coöperating with the Municipal Art Commission, two members of which belong to the Ruskin Club. The Municipal

Art Commission is seeking in many ways to beautify the city and is greatly interested in securing the services of a city architect who will lay out the plan for the greater Los Angeles.

What has been said touching the civic and philanthropic interest shown by the women of Los Angeles, whose organizations have already been described, may also be said of the many women of the other clubs throughout the city. In these days of altruistic effort, the women who give time to mere amusement clubs are missing much that makes life worth living. The way in which the women of Los Angeles gave themselves to service on the various relief boards after the San Francisco disaster, speaks well for the future of this city. If the same amount of earnest work were given year by year along all lines of helpful service, marvelous results would be accomplished. What might not the women of this city do in keeping open the door of hope for the fallen sisters, in working earnestly in the cause of child labor? The toiling sister in our modern industrialism needs not only friends, but she needs also those who will study her problems and set in motion the forces which will finally bring relief.

Banded together for God and Home and Everyland, the W. C. T. U. of Los Angeles is said to have the largest membership of any single union in the world. It is making warfare against "the one great wasting destroying

force of human life." It has greatly broadened
the scope of its work so as to include agitation,
education, legislation and moral suasion.
Through a score of departments, it touches in
a helpful way many sides of life. It places
stress on methods which make for the destruction of the liquor traffic; the training of parents in the value of prenatal influence, that
every child may be well born, and in raising
the standard of purity until public sentiment
may demand "a white life for two." This band
of great-hearted women who compose this organization have put their hands to large tasks,
and have already won great victories in their
warfare against deadly evils.

Many of the young women of Los Angeles
are busy in the various activities of the Young
Women's Christian Association—the largest in
the world in point of numbers, having an en-
rollment of over 4,000. Engaged in the promotion of education and in sustaining arts,
they easily attract wage earners who desire to
better their condition and at the same time
have the help and fellowship of noble women.
The noon-day lunch, patronized by over 1,100
women, brings the Association well on the way
to self support. In coöperation with the Deaconess' Association, the Y. W. C. A. maintains
three Travelers-aid Deaconesses at the depots,
who meet all unattended women, directing
them to friends or boarding places, and furnishing them aid and care when needed. Vari-

"EL NIDO," THE HOME OF MADAME SEVERANCE

ous clubs maintain rest rooms near the Arcade
Depot, and cottages at the beaches. The
rapid growth of this Association called for a
large and well-equipped building, now under
erection, which is destined to touch for good
the lives of a multitude of young women, many
of whom may be far from home and friends.

The publication of the autobiography of a
working girl, entitled "The Long Day," has
drawn attention to the fearful condition of the
average working girl, who receives so small a
wage that she cannot afford to live in a decent
place where she can find a home or lodging.
As a result of this aroused interest, there will
no doubt be built by the Y. W. C. A., Salvation
Army and other kindred organizations, hotels
for women, similar to the existing men's hotels,
thus protecting the working girl, who is in far
greater danger than the young man away from
home and its helpful influence.

From all these various activities it is evident
that the women of the city are well organized
for social and civic betterment, and it goes
without saying that they will prove to be a
growing factor in the making of the Better
City.

8

CHAPTER VI.

THE CHILD IN THE MIDST

The Great Teacher said of old, "Let the little children come to me, and do not hinder them, for it is to the child-like that the Kingdom of Heaven belongs." When the new ideal society of which he spoke is at last established, the child will be in the midst, and be of all citizens the most honored. The world's noblest souls will be the teachers of the child; learned specialists will give instruction as to the value of prenatal influences, so that a clean, healthy parenthood may be the boon of every child. Psychologists will give popular lectures on the power of suggestion and environment upon young life; and on the moral and spiritual value of the adolescent period. Religious teachers will seek for the fullest development of the soul life. The State as the good Over-father of all will seek not merely to punish the wayward, but to bring all into the highest citizenship.

The greatest study of man is not man full grown, but man in the making. It is easier to form than to reform; easier to start a tree right than to straighten it when full grown. It is more economical to train up a child in the right way than to punish and reform him as a delinquent when full grown. The world is yet far from the ideal. Birth, environment, instruction are oftentimes all bad. Yet despite all drawbacks, child workers report great progress toward the ideal.

Among the child-saving agencies, the first in importance is the home. The influence of a good home never dies; though the son become a prodigal, sooner or later, the song of home and mother will awaken echoes of a happier past and bring him back to the better life. But all children are not born in real homes. The tenement with its foul and dark rooms, never tempts a child to stay indoors, but sends him out into the courtyard and street for social life and companionship. The slatternly, loud-voiced mother who was sorry when the child was born, never inspires to clean living. The father, drunken and profane, is at first feared, and afterwards imitated. Considered from the standpoint of the child, the housing problem takes on significance. Destroy the tenement, scatter the population, encourage the growing of plants and vines, and the new environment will give the child a fair chance and may be the means of the reform of the parents as well.

Untrained and ignorant, many do not know the value of good thoughts and pure living to the unborn child. The science of eugenics may yet aid in giving us a race all "well born." May not the State claim the right and the duty to say that mental and physical defectives shall not be allowed to propagate their kind? Reacting upon home life, the kindergarten is as useful for the parent as the child. The permeating influence of education succeeds when all other agencies fail. The Mother's Club in the School and Settlement furnish ideals for home transformation. Temperance reform purifies civic life; good reading, elevating entertainments, and new spiritual ideals have their bearing on the uplifting of home life and therefore on the saving of the child.

Our hearts are always moved by the sight of the unfortunate and the abnormal. Yet the great mass of children are above that line and are normal in their development. For such the public school spells power. The three h's —the head, the heart, and the hand—are supplementing the three R's, resulting more and more in the harmonious development of the body, mind and spirit.

It was Plato who advised the putting out of the way all the weak and imbecile children, as well as the aged when they became a burden. This was a survival of the fittest, which is the law in the animal world. The making fit to survive is more Godlike. Under the power of this new idea, the strong are giving of their strength to the weak, soul touching soul until healing virtue passes into the darkened mind. The miracle of the new birth is witnessed daily in the school and institution as well as in the church and cathedral. The story of man's part in this wonderful soul awakening is thrilling in the extreme. There is for example the story of the physician who spent hours with the poor imbecile until the dawning of consciousness made it possible for others to carry on the development; or the story of the noble woman whose life devotion to the mute blind girl was rewarded by seeing her develop into that woman of rare powers, Helen Keller. These and a multitude of others that might be mentioned, are altruistic heroes, whose recompense does not consist in money or medals, but in consciousness of being workers with the Divine in the wonderful process of re-creation. The mental and the physical defectives cannot be destroyed. The amount of science, knowledge and love applied to their restoration is the measure of our best civilization.

In the ordinary rush of modern commercialism, the weaklings—children and adults as well—are being forced to the wall, to become paupers or the wards of the State. The new day has a new spirit. The recovery of defectives to citizenship and power is part of the program of those whose souls are stirred by the thought of universal love and a truer manhood.

There are perhaps about 180,000 defective children in this country, waiting for some one to love them back into normal life. I say "love," for that is the secret of the success. The teacher of the abnormal child needs love and still more love, for after years of experiment, it is shown that love opens all avenues to the soul. A striking example of that is given in "The American Motherhood," in the story of the awakening of Sylvanus. Sylvanus was an imbecile eight years old. Mr. James B. Richards says, "I got down on the floor beside the child, and day after day for six months read to him as though he understood every word. One day I read to myself, and Sylvanus lifted his finger and laid it on my lips." He had expressed a want, a beginning at least of the final recovery. Years of such loving treatment passed by, and little by little the light broke into the darkened mind. Seeing a child with its mother, Sylvanus asked one day, "Have I a mother?" She was sent for, and when she came, he said, "O mother, I am so glad to see you." A soul had been liberated at last through love. Does it pay to spend so much more money upon the abnormal than upon the normal? Ask the father of the child, helpless for years, who was brought back to the joyous play of childhood by the skill of Prof. Lorenz. Ask the mother of the child, deaf, dumb and blind, who has been taught to read and speak and take his part in the family life. Get the testimony of a thousand homes made happy by the return to them of bright, happy children, once feeble in mind and body.

At Eldridge Home, 300 of California's 2,000 or 3,000 feeble-minded folk are cared for. In some of the best institutions in the country seventy-five per cent are regarded as teachable and given constant attention under scientific supervision. Much is made of farm work, the growing of flowers, and the various forms of industrial work. There are no punishments, but a system of rewards for work well done. In the best of schools, thirty per cent of the inmates can be made self-supporting in ten years. The girls of the school make, repair and laundry the clothes for all; the boys do the farm work and are employed in many trades and help in the house work. One can see that only the best teachers should be used in such schools. "The duller the child, the better the teacher must be and more love and enthusiasm must he have for the work."

The movement in public school life for medical inspection is showing that many backward children are so not because of mental failure, but because of impaired eyesight, partial deafness, physical malformation or nervous disturbance. When these troubles are remedied, they become like other normal children. For those who are backward, many cities have provided special schools where the children receive individual instruction and in this way are enabled to keep up with their grades.

No work for children has called out so much sympathy and philanthropic effort as the care of orphans and dependent children. According to a late report, there are in California 5,852 dependent children, in 44 asylums. Of these, 1,005 are orphans; 4,133, half orphans; 469, abandoned children; 228, foundlings; while 2,481 children are cared for by the State outside of institutions. The orphanages maintain about 1,200 children who do not receive State aid, but whose maintenance is provided for by relatives and friends.*

Dependent children are kept in institutions on the congregate plan, divided among cottages, or boarded out in homes found for them. Each plan has its advocates, though the institutional plan, except as a temporary resort, is much less in favor than formerly. While all dependent children are considered as wards of the State, California, unlike some Eastern States, has no institution of its own. With the exception of a County orphanage at Fresno, all of the remaining forty-three are private benevolent establishments, fifteen of them being under the Catholic Church, the remainder under Protestant control or belonging to benevolent orders. The objection to congregating children in large institutions is founded on the result of such treatment. Well-fed, healthy children though they are, saved from bad habits and usually taught religion, they are often found lacking in the power of initiative, push and independence and that development of individualism which is so necessary to success in this world. The individual has been assim-

*Institutional Life. Arthur J. Pillsbury.

THE CATHOLIC ORPHANS' ASYLUM

ilated in the mass, and has become institution-alized. A prominent social worker, after watching a large group of well-fed orphans march to the table in perfect silence and move on through all the day as one mass, said, "It is an awful thing to see 400 children behaving at once." It is a human deed to save the orphan child from the peril of the streets, but in these days philanthropy cannot stop at that, but ought to seek to aid in the fullest develop-ment of every child. A self-reliant independent personality is the product sought for.

As an ordinary home is better than any orphanage, the nearer to the home life the orphanage can be brought, the better it will be. The cottage plan, while more costly than the congregate, is much better because more nat-ural; every cottage, neat, attractive, and home-like, having its house mother or father and from twenty to twenty-five children. This group resembles a well-ordered family, each doing a part for the good of all. Where pos-sible, the children should attend the public school, going and coming like other children. If situated in the country, the daily work upon the farm and in the flower garden will be a great aid in the normal development. There will exist a friendly rivalry among the children as to whose cottage shall be the most home-like and attractive, whose yard shall be the brightest with flowers and vines. Believing that a home is better than an institution, some states have adopted a plan for boarding out the children. In Massachusetts, where asylums are privately endowed, the state furnishes no further aid, but looks after dependent children not in institutions, and boards out in private families some 4,000 children. Beside providing clothing and medical aid, it pays from $2.00 to $2.75 per week for board. All homes are carefully investigated, and the children looked after by fifty volunteer visitors, and by a force of trained visitors who devote their time to the work. Boston does an independent work, having 900 children scattered through the New England States, looked after by paid visitors. Pennsylvania regards the boarding-out plan as better than that of the institution. The Aid Society of Philadelphia receives children whose parents have encountered industrial hardships, through strikes or lockouts or lack of work, and boards them out among the farmers at $1.50 or $2.75 per week, allowing $30 per year for clothing and bringing them back again when the parents are able to support them. Ofttimes the farmers are so unwilling to give up these children that arrangements are made for their further stay, without the payment of any board. Of the 7,000 boarded out, 3,000 are on such a free list.

This system will not work of itself, but must be safeguarded by constant visits to the homes, so as to protect the children from ill treatment and overwork. Owing to the present-day con-

ditions, economical and social, there are many
thousand homes without any child life. It is safe
to say that there is a homeless child for every
childless home; to bring these two together is
as much a problem as to get the landless man
on the manless land. All states are now interested in placing, as speedily as possible, all
the uncared-for children in some good home,
provided they cannot be returned to their relatives. Every county in Michigan employs a
special agent who places dependents in homes,
visiting and reporting regularly to the State.
The Children's Home Society makes a special
point of finding suitable homes throughout the
West. The Children's Aid Society is the oldest of the home-finding societies, having placed
tens of thousands, with a bad report on only
five per cent. The problem is how to get the
homeless child to the childless home soon
enough to secure for it the loving embrace of
the woman with the mother's heart before it
becomes fixed in the ways of institutional life.
All children in the institution are not ideal.
There is need of those who with unselfish con-
secration are willing to take the unpromising
children and do their part for society by loving
them into decent manhood and womanhood.
Not enough can be said against the purely
selfish desire which seeks an orphan for adoption either because of its beauty or attractive-
ness or because of future ability as a worker,
thus saving the hire of a servant.

By placing the emphasis upon home finding for dependent children social workers are not saying that there is no need for the institution. Temporary care ofttimes is all that is necessary. For instance, until the widow or the widower marries again, or the former secures remunerative employment where she will be able to support the child, there is need for such care. The average length of institutional life in California for such is between two and three years. Another use of the asylum is to prepare for home life by the removing of all physical defects and handicaps, by straightening crooked limbs and removing adenoid growths. Special emphasis is laid upon this work in the institutions in Iowa, Michigan, Massachusetts and New York. Institutions will always be necessary in order to care for unattractive children whom no one wants, of whom it is reckoned there are about 1,000 in California asylums. The "basket baby" is always in evidence. What is the best thing to do with such foundlings? In the ordinary asylum, the death rate of the little ones has been from fifty to ninty-eight per cent. In order to avoid this dreadful mortality, this state gives $12.50 a month to have the children boarded out under the care of a good mother, where they can obtain plenty of fresh cow's milk. New York has found that among Italian women accustomed to the service of midwives, two-fifths of the infants are still born. By

placing the foundlings with these healthy
mothers, they are well cared for until they
are able to stand the life of an institution.
California believes that "aid in the home of a
surviving and worthy parent is the best form
of state aid." Many are cared for who never
enter an institution. This state believes in
the family unit, and is determined not to have
the family broken up simply because of poverty. After a careful study of conditions
throughout the country, Mr. Pillsbury writes:
"Eastern states in general say in effect to the
widowed mother, 'Very well, madam, if you
cannot support your children, we will take
them from you and parcel them out to persons
who can support them, but they will no longer
be your children. They will be adopted by
others and will become as much their children
as if born to them.' California says to such
an unfortunate woman, 'Madam, the state
sympathizes with you in your distress and is
ready and willing to help you reasonably. You
may place the children in the orphanage of
your choice and leave them there, visiting them
meantime on proper occasions, until you develop an earning capacity which will enable
you to get them under a roof of your own
providing. Or they may remain under your
own roof, if you have one, and through your
local supervisors you may receive as much
state aid as you need and no more, provided
that it does not exceed $75 per year, and you

may receive that aid as long as you need it and no longer. You may thus keep your family together without grave hardship and your children will belong to you and not to a stranger.' The heart of California is right; and it is better to submit to some imposition than that in the name of economy, the state should steel its heart against the fundamental promptings of parental affection."

Fifty years ago, the Sisters of Charity came to this city from the Mother House in Maryland, and established an asylum on Alameda Street. Later they built their large and attractive Home on Boyle Heights. There are now 350 girls who are orphans, half orphans, or abandoned, under their constant care, their entire training, spiritual, physical and mental being given within the building. The Los Angeles Orphan's Home, founded twenty-four years ago, has a substantial brick building on Alpine Street. One hundred and fifty children receive the usual care, together with instruction in sloyd and manual training. In addition they have the very great privilege of attending the public school in the neighborhood, the older children also being allowed to attend the nearby churches on Sunday. The Boy's and Girl's Home in South Pasadena has about 125 bright boys and girls. This institution is on the congregate plan. The latest asylum to be founded is that of the Volunteers of America on Twenty-third Street and Vermont

Avenue. This was opened just in time to receive the thirty-two orphans brought from the San Francisco House after the fire. While all of these institutions seek permanent homes for the children, the McKinley Home for boys is the only one which has adopted the cottage plan. Situated on a farm about half way to the ocean, it offers an ideal place for the training of the eighty boys gathered under its roof. Manual training, flowers, gardens, public school instruction, and the appointment of house mothers make it quite up-to-date in the working out of the cottage plan. All of these institutions receive state aid, and whenever possible, regular payments from relatives, besides donation from friends. At no time, however, are they without the need of more financial help. State aid for the child ceases at fourteen years. But what shall become of the children after that age when they are turned out into the world without fitness for self-support? If the asylum cannot follow them through their critical years, the state should keep them under its watchful care and introduce a system of visitation and work finding to aid them until they are well able to care for themselves. It is the purpose of the Newsboys' Home in this city to receive working boys over fourteen and thus tide over this critical time. They have now two cottages in use.

It is a question how much philanthropy

helps to solve the problems of the world. But so long as there are forces at work producing conditions which make for poverty and dependency, no one will deny that it is a splendid charity to care for the children of mothers who, because of the death or abandonment of their husbands, are forced to work, and by such care make it possible to keep the family together until the dawning of a better day. The King's Daughters' Day Nursery started in the Bethlehem Church in 1895, has now built a commodious house on Clarence Street to carry on that work. At Manhattan Beach, in their pleasant rest cottage, forty children have received a whole month's outing each year. The Children's Home Society on East Twenty-fifth Street has received 126 children for the year, and has permanently placed eighty-eight in selected homes.

But our debt to society is not discharged by caring for the feeble and the dependent little ones. The delinquents—those who have done wrong, must be recovered, or the jails of the future will be filled and society will be the loser. It is only a few years since the public conscience was aroused in regard to the treatment of juvenile delinquents. Before that, all children were arrested like adult criminals, driven to jails in patrol wagons, thrown into cells, tried in the same court, sentenced to the jail or the penitentiary, or at best to the reform school. These were all schools of crime, out

LOS ANGELES ORPHANS' HOME

of which the children came as graduates. But now the child is in the midst, and his value to the state is fully recognized. He is no longer looked upon as a criminal fit only for reformation; he is looked upon as an unfortunate child needing formation and direction. In most of our cities, the delinquent child is now placed in a detention home rather than in a jail. He has a court of his own, presided over by a kind-hearted judge. He is not sentenced to imprisonment, but placed under a probation officer who helps him with respect to his home, his school or his work, and to whom he must report, for he is a ward of the Court. Only when he is found to be incorrigible is he sent to the reform school. Gradually the old type of penitentiary-like reform school is giving place to the cottage plan on the distant farm, or to the finding of farm work for groups under a probation officer or to a speedy parole for good behavior. Many states prefer to place their delinquents among farmers in the same way as they do their dependents. It is usually conceded that under the new Juvenile Court law, eighty-one per cent of all brought before the Court are benefited and saved to society, while under the old system, ninety-five per cent were lost. A long list of up-to-date institutions could be given, where the highest thought for child training is being put into practice. Notably in this list of helpful agencies may be mentioned the "George Junior Republic," es-

9

tablished by Mr. W. R. George at Freeville,
N. Y. This is self-governing and eminently
successful. In response to an invitation from
the Juvenile Court Association, Mr. George
came to Los Angeles this spring and aroused
considerable interest and enthusiasm for this
kind of work, leaving the social workers determined to raise $25,000 for the beginning of a
similar work near this city. The credit is to
be given to Colorado for establishing the principle that he who contributes to the delinquency of a child is himself a delinquent. Under the law, the men who sell liquor or cigarettes to children are brought into Court and
fined or sent to jail. In the same way tele-
graph and messenger companies are brought
into Court for sending boys to immoral places.
A stop has thus been put in Colorado to a
custom still in practice in Los Angeles, where
boys are freely sent to the worst of places.
It is to be hoped that this principle of adult
responsibility may soon be universally applied.

Among the new methods of dealing with
delinquents, that of medical examination and
treatment as an aid to moral recovery is com-
mendable. In Philadelphia specialists are now
at work with ten thousand children from the
poorer districts, removing physical defects,
which are in many instances said to be the direct cause of the criminal instinct that lead
them into sin. Already wonderful results have
been obtained.

In the Juvenile Court of Los Angeles, Judge Wilbur is seeking to apply all the new ideas indicated, with much success. He is ably assisted by the Juvenile Court Committee, five probation officers and fifty deputy officers. The chief drawback has been the lack of a suitable Detention Home, the old jail with its atmosphere of crime being used temporarily. It is to be hoped that very soon this city will have a thoroughly equipped Detention Home, in connection with which there shall be no suggestion of police court or jail.

The question of truancy and child labor is closely associated with the work of the Juvenile Court. In order to separate the mere truant from the vicious child, the Board of Education has opened two special schools for truants or mischief makers, and has bought a beautiful site north of Elysian Park for a parental school—the city standing in the place of a parent. This will be the first parental school in the state, and will aid materially in lessening the number of future criminals.

The Juvenile Court Committee has organized an Association to extend the opportunities of the Court in its efforts to help individual children, and to bring the public into active coöperation with the Juvenile Court. The work of the Association has been outlined as follows: "To provide the money for the successful conducting of such parts of the work of the Court as must necessarily be maintained by private expenditure. Poverty, sickness and evil surroundings place the children in the gravest peril, demanding prompt relief in manifold ways.

"To aid in the gradual development of a system of special probation officers and in the securing by legislation or otherwise of an increase in the number of deputy probation officers.

"To take active part in the study of conditions and in the effort to secure the betterment of conditions for children. To reach the group of boys, to find and remedy the cause of a certain bad condition, whether local or far-reaching—this is child saving far beyond the possibilities that lie in the Juvenile Court, content to 'do its best' with each individual child brought before it for dependency or delinquency.

"Therefore, all over the land, among the progressive people working to help children, will be found this eagerness, not only to help the individual child, but to go farther and find the cause of the child's sad state and deal with it to an extent made possible only by strong support and intelligent interest."

Membership in the Association was sought from all churches, clubs and other organizations willing to contribute $25 annually, and individuals willing to contribute $5. Regarding the establishment of this Association, Judge Wilbur of the Juvenile Court writes as follows: "I desire to say in regard to the work of the Juvenile Court that I am more than persuaded, as I see the way in which the work of the Court enters into the life of the people, that the Juvenile Court idea will form the rallying point about which almost all of the measures of reform with regard to the education and training of the child life will center. The problem of the Juvenile Court is as large as life itself. It is obvious therefore that the intelligence of a large number of people is essential to the proper conduct of the work. Touching human life and activity at all points as does the Juvenile Court, through the probation officers, it is obvious that there must be an elasticity which is impossible under any law, and as can only exist by the helpful coöperation of those who are willing to devote time and money to the upbuilding of humanity. I have said comparatively little with reference to the question of money in dealing with the problem of the Juvenile Court, yet the fact that the Whittier State School is being depopulated, resulting in a large saving to the taxpayers, is significant. Los Angeles City is today being taxed over $600,000 to support insane asylums, states prisons, jails, sheriffs, police and homes for the feeble minded children, yearly. I know of no way in which money can be so well used to stem this awful drain as in the work of caring for these children who are so far dependent or delinquent as to come before the Juvenile Court."

While there is very much new work inaugurated on behalf of child life, the older agencies are ever busy. The Sunday School, Junior Societies, Bands of Hope and Mercy, Humane Societies, Boy's Clubs and Brigades, Y. M. C. A. athletics and night schools, industrial and trade schools, fresh-air work, children's hospitals, kindergarten and child-study circles are all working with loving purpose. All such efforts on behalf of the child in the midst will surely aid in the creation of the Better City.

CHAPTER VII.

POSITIVE TEMPERANCE

The American saloon is the great hindrance in the upbuilding of the Better City. It not only debauches many of the citizens, lessening their earning power, making them less able to resist disease, breaking up their home life, producing among them poverty and pauperism; but entering into politics it becomes a standing menace to better city government. President Roosevelt has well said that "the liquor traffic tends to produce criminality in the population at large, and law breaking among the saloon keepers themselves." If the saloon is an institution harmful to the best interests of the modern city, be it remembered that every city has the right to regulate or even prohibit it. The Supreme Court has decided that "to sell liquor is not one of the rights growing out of citizenship in the United States." And again, "there is no inherent right of a citizen thus to sell liquors by retail. It is not a privilege of the citizen of the State or the citizen of the United States." The question of regulation or prohibition of the saloon is being continually brought before every city seeking the best interests of its citizens. In this connection an

epoc-making decision has been recently
handed down by Judge Samuel Artman of the
Circuit Court of Indiana, in refusing to allow
the granting of a saloon license. He held that
the State cannot delegate to the saloon a legal
existence under the guise of a license, in that
a saloon leads to immorality, suffering and
loss of life.

Is it any wonder that in the majority of
American municipalities there is a strong sentiment toward greater and still greater restrictions upon the traffic, until its final ex-
tinction has been secured? Many convinced
that it is a check upon the highest progress
are ready to ask with Dr. Robert Burdette:
"Can you name one good thing the saloon
has done for humanity—one good thing—but
one instance in which it has brought forth
fruit unto righteousness—one influence, sweet
and healthful and pure and gracious and beautiful, which will linger lovingly in the mem-
ory of men, when you have buried the rum
power to make them say, 'God bless the saloon for the good it did?' Search through
the history of this hateful thing and try to
discover one page over which a mother can
bow her grateful head and thank God for all
the saloon did for her boy. There is no such
record. All its history is written in tears and
blood, with smears of shame, and stains of
crime, and dark blots of disgrace." It would
be bad enough if the evil were to end with the

YOUNG WOMENS' CHRISTIAN ASSOCIATION BUILDING, LOS ANGELES.

Y. W. C. A. NEW BUILDING

adults now being ruined in the American saloon, but it is an acknowledged fact that the combined liquor element is seeking to ensnare the boys who are to be the men of the next generation. To the educator, the Juvenile Court worker, the settlement resident, and to all lovers of boys, this fact is most serious in its consequences and far reaching in its results. The author, born in Maine and brought up in Iowa, was a grown man before he had ever seen a saloon or the color of any liquor. So far as he knows, not one of his schoolmates ever became a drinking man. What he enjoyed for himself, he desires for every other boy in the land—a chance to grow up in a clean city and a pure atmosphere.

No city ever afforded a more striking example of the good result of saloon suppression than did the once saloon-cursed San Francisco, when after the fire every saloon was closed. A Chronicle editorial described it as a city almost without crime. It said: "San Francisco for the past fortnight has been absolutely free from disorder and virtually free from crimes of violence. There have been no street brawls. No drunken brute has murdered his wife. No gamblers have murdered each other in low resorts. Except for some dealings with sneak thieves, the occupation of the police is gone. It is an impressive object lesson of the value to society of the restriction of the liquor traffic." The same paper declared that when the saloons were opened, many former drinkers after seventy-nine days of abstinence seemed cured of the cocktail habit. "Liquor drinking," it added, "is with most people not the gratification of an appetite, but a mere habit. There is no liquor and few wines which taste good. Even the toper who takes his whiskey straight washes the taste out of his mouth with water as quickly as he can. With a comparatively few there is a real craving for liquor, or at least its stimulating effects, but the vast majority of those who drink in the saloons do so merely because in the poverty of their intellects they do not know of any other way of manifesting good fellowship toward friends whom they meet. So the drink habit is formed, which in many cases degenerates into dissipation and the drunkard's craving."

The story of the liquor regulation in Los Angeles shows what can be done largely through the education of public opinion. Los Angeles is an American city, being to a great extent made up of those who came first as tourists from the East and Middle West, and fascinated by the conditions of life in this Sunny Land have returned as citizens. It is a city of churches and schools and civic bodies, deeply interested in creating the best. The type is that of the highest moral and ethical citizenship. In 1899 the Council passed an ordinance limiting the number of saloons to

200 and prohibiting their extension into the residence districts. While the liquor traffic has continually fought this ordinance, it still remains the law of the city, notwithstanding that the city has more than doubled in population. While the laws regulating the control of the saloon have not always been enforced, each year has seen more restrictive measures passed, such as the removal of chairs, boxes and tables, and the prohibition of women and minors from the saloons. The matter of bringing the numerous social clubs of the city under city control is now under discussion. Under the present law, the police have no more power of inspection over these than they have over a private residence.

Among the forces at work creating public sentiment, the Anti-saloon League is prominent. This organization under the able leadership of Dr. E. S. Chapman, has within the last few years succeeded in changing the black map of Southern California into a white map with black spots. By means of local option campaigns in both township and county, six counties are now dry, with the exception of one or two towns, while outside of Los Angeles, fifty-five of the towns and cities in Southern California are dry. These campaigns carry on educational propaganda through platform and press so that the vote is an intelligent one. At the last election the roadhouses outside the city were voted out, so that there is neither roadhouse nor licensed saloon within a radius of ten miles beyond the city limits, except in a few places where the supervisors have granted special privileges. The work of saloon suppression was so successful outside of the cities in 1904, that the Anti-saloon League organized its forces for a campaign in Los Angeles. After a hard-fought contest, the temperance people were defeated.

There are many other organizations at work for temperance in this city. The Prohibition party is ever active, seeking the entire overthrow of the liquor traffic. The Good Templars maintain a number of lodges, and are helpful on the side of positive temperance. John Sobieski, the lineal descendant of King John Sobieski of Poland, is an honored resident of this city who labors constantly for temperance on the lecture platform. Francis Murphy, the leader for so many years of the blue-ribbon movement, but who closed his eventful life on June 30th, was another citizen of Los Angeles, who gave his life to this good work, securing thousands of signatures to the total abstinence pledge. The W. C. T. U. has here the largest federation in the entire country. Through their many lines of work and education, they have exerted a very decided influence on the side of positive temperance. The Catholic Society, known as the Father Mathew Society, the Salvation Army, the Volunteers of America, and the Rescue Missions recover many who have formed the drink habit, and save many who have just started on the downward way. The Y. M. C. A. is now building a character factory costing $350,000. This movement will furnish a positive factor in the temperance work, providing as it does, lodgings, reading rooms, baths, educational and athletic facilities, thus making for a full rounded life, and standing for self-control in all things. The new Y. W. C. A. building with its enlarged facilities will also enable that organization to do for the women what the Y. M. C. A. does for the men. In all the churches of the city there is a great awakening of interest along social lines, with a consequent arousing of zeal for temperance, in proportion as the people come to realize the relation between good social conditions and the temperate life. Whenever a public official is found who courageously enforces the existing laws, great progress is made in any reform. District Attorney J. D. Fredericks, after serving a term in office in which he enforced the liquor laws without fear or favor, was re-elected by an overwhelming majority, showing that the people believe in such law enforcement.

While rejoicing in definite campaigns conducted against the liquor traffic with such success, and in the passage and enforcement of laws restricting the traffic, we must not forget that a vast amount of good work is being done which is not negative or prohibitory, but is positive in its methods. The creating of saloon substitutes—the furnishing of ordinary education, the teaching of a trade, the creation of a love for good reading, the work of home building, the teaching of the value of foods and the proper methods of cooking them, in short everything which arouses the best in a man and helps him to break the bondage of mere appetite and passions, tends in the direction of positive temperance. Power from within is worth more than restraint from without. The extension of education to the training in the actual doing of things, as well as in the three R's, resulting in the awakening of genius and in the preparing for a life work adapted to each child is also tributary to this end. The kindergarten has its reflex influence upon the home, in teaching nature's order, and in including thoughtfulness for another's interests. The cooking school helps to make good housewives, and good food is a strong promoter of temperance. The bath tub, the school nurse, the gymnasium and the playground all help in creating a vigorous physical life with great vitality and power of resistance which does not call for stimulants, but is content with the simple life.

The newest movement in connection with the public school also has its bearing on temperance. This movement consists in making the school a community center where night schools are held, open to the young and middle aged alike, where popular lectures are given, and where thousands of men may spend a profitable evening away from the contaminating influence of the saloon. The Child Study Circles reaching as they do so many mothers from among the poor, offer another avenue for temperance instruction.

Far reaching as is the public school in its temperance instruction and indirect influence, the public library is now vieing with it in bringing the light. The intellectual, artistic and industrial progress of a community can be aided by a larger use of our public libraries, and according to reports many libraries have adopted aggressive measures in order to stimulate the use of the books which fill their shelves. They supplement the work of the public schools. They minister to industrial needs. Their books on useful and fine arts are in constant demand. They distribute books through day schools, Sunday Schools, clubs, firehouses and other convenient agencies. They circulate catalogues and leaflets in factories and stores. They hold special exhibits. They send out thousands of postal cards calling attention to new books. They make their contents easy of access, and furthermore, in order to increase steadily the number of regular patrons mailing cards with an invitation to use the library are sent out each week to persons selected from the city directory. In this way many are led to read good books, and time outside of work hours which offers so many temptations is well used, and the higher nature stimulated.

Many of the leading business men not only set before their employees a good example of total abstinence, but insist that their workmen shall not frequent saloons. This attitude is now recognized as an economic necessity. An extract from a letter of C. P. Huntington shows the result in the building of the Central Pacific Railroad: "I have no doubt that it would have taken three or four, perhaps five, years longer to build the Central Pacific Railroad if we had allowed drinking saloons on the ground, but we took that matter in hand ourselves and did not allow any deadfalls along the line. After the work had reached Yuba, about twenty-five miles from Dutch Flat, we then took control and drove all of that class of people away, and were not disturbed between there and Salt Lake, but before that these institutions followed us and we could not prevent it, as we could not control them, and the result was that on Mondays we would have but a few men at work; Tuesdays, something more; and not until Thursday as it were would we have anything like a full force at work, and the balance who did work were more or less demoralized by these institutions." Today factories not only enforce the rule prohibiting their employees from entering saloons, but they are giving more and more

Y. M. C. A. NEW BUILDING

attention to "welfare work," within their own establishments. Under the leadership of S. E. Busser, the Santa Fe has applied the Golden Rule to railroading by providing at all division points "incentives for the railroad boys to be good and keep their heads clear and save their money, to sleep in sanitary, decent quarters, to indulge in sane recreation, and keep away from the bar-room and the gambling joint — building up a higher individuality and thus making for greater efficiency." Here again in these reading rooms and meeting places is a positive power at work for temperance. In line with this movement is the custom followed by many business men of granting the Saturday half holiday, a thing which makes it possible for the working man during the summer months to take his family to a seaside resort, free from the temptations of the city saloons.

The movement for the establishment of social centers should be encouraged, not alone because of their educational value but because they furnish meeting places where the social instincts can be gratified without any of the evils of questionable resorts. The building of Civic Centers such as those in the South Park in Chicago encourages living the normal life free from the excitement of the guilded palaces of sin.

That man is a gregarious animal is a fact to be recognized by all reformers. It is not

10

enough to close the saloon. If nothing better is offered, a man will seek "a hole in the wall" in an alley, provided that it is a place where others may be found. Have we thought sufficiently of the plight of the young man in the hall bedroom? Away from friends, he is more alone in the great city than in a desert. After work and supper at a chop house, he tries to read in his own room, but soon the intolerable loneliness of it gets on his nerves. He wanders to and fro on the streets, drawn tonight into a cheap theater, tomorrow night into a dance hall, after that into the brightly lighted saloon. He has no intention of doing anything wrong, but where else can he go? The few friends that he has made are no help to him and he even loses his grip on all of his better purposes. For the sake of the hall bedroom young man, close the saloon! Yes, but give him something better. If the Y. M. C. A. could have a number of widely scattered points of contact in addition to these in the one great center, this young man might not be so lonely. If all the churches were churches of the open door, there would be more young men in their congregations. If there were a systematic effort to seek out continually the young man in his lodging house, and invite him to home and friends, many a life would be saved.

As a substitute for the saloon, the Coffee Club is very effective. Those of the Coffee

Club Association in Los Angeles, and of the Bethlehem Institution are always filled to overflowing. Undoubtedly many of their frequenters are homeless men who might otherwise be found in the saloon. The Bethlehem Men's Hotels furnish not only a gathering place, but also a homelike atmosphere, with music and entertainments, thus ministering to the entire man. But there are men who have low tastes and who do not feel at home in the Y. M. C. A. or Coffee Club, where as a daily paper says, "they will not be allowed to light their pipes, put their feet on the table, lean back in their chairs and blow smoke rings to the ceiling. . . . Men wish to assemble in public places where there is entire freedom as to dress and appearance, and where there is no danger that anyone will solicit them to become better men. They are not only willing, but desire to spend something for the 'good of the house' and for their own entertainment. If society will provide them with such a place, a good many will go there in preference to the saloon. If at the same time, all saloons were abolished, they will speedily content themselves with the substitutes such as we have suggested."

All reforms are bound together in a common purpose and the success or failure of one affects all the others. We hold that the Housing Commission is also a Temperance Commission, and that the Sanitary Engineer is not so far removed from his friend of the Anti-saloon League. Any woman who works for the creation of the City Beautiful is in her efforts related to the white-ribboner. Still more closely related to one another are those who work for saloon suppression and those who are giving their thought and energy to the securing of a change in economic conditions. Break the power of the dollar, and you close both the saloon and the brothel. The Whiskey Trust is making millions out of these trades, and stands in the way of law enforcement. They must make drunkards or they cannot sell their goods. A writer has well put it: "Drunkenness is not an isolated disease but the direct product of the social conditions, and it cannot be cured apart from these conditions." What then are some of the next steps toward saloon suppression to be taken in Los Angeles, in addition to law enforcement and a campaign of education? We answer without hesitation, "The opening of more such centers as those furnished by the Bethlehem Institute and the Coffee Clubs, and the establishment of an adequate number of public comfort stations." Many thousands are led to drink through patronizing the saloons for the use of the toilet privileges.

Twenty-two of the prominent business men of the city have offered to establish the Gothenburg System to replace the ordinary saloon. It is their plan to ask the city to vote on the question, and if the vote is favorable, to have the liquor business turned over to them. They would then close all but seventy saloons; all of those in the residence and industrial districts, substituting coffee clubs where necessary; they would take but six per cent for their dividends, all surplus going to the city; and they would see that the laws are strictly enforced. The bar keeper would have no interest in increasing the sale of intoxicating liquors, his commission being on soft drinks; treating would be discouraged; secrecy would be done away with, the stores being without screens; the power of the dollar would be largely eliminated, and the business taken out of politics. Unlike the original Gothenburg plan, this would include the wine and beer saloons, which the former did not include. Before this scheme is submitted to the people, it has been thought best to submit the entire liquor problem to a committee of prominent citizens who shall decide whether to suggest this plan at all or to reduce still further the number of saloons and narrow the saloon zone, adopting more stringent laws regulating the time and methods of sale. Whatever may be the decision of this group of men, the temperance workers will not cease night or day in their efforts to lessen the power of the liquor traffic, and thus help to make a Better City.

CHAPTER VIII.

SEEKING HEALTH

In creating a city, due regard must be given to the preservation of health and the prevention of contagion. The mosquito with its yellow fever virus, the typhoid germ, malaria and the tuberculosis bacillus must be fought and conquered. The solving of the sewerage problem is as important to health and happiness of the people as the building of hospitals and boulevards. Sanitary buildings are of greater importance to health than Grecian architecture. The death rate of the city does not depend on an over-ruling Providence as much as it does on the care and far-sightedness of the city fathers. The owner of an unsanitary tenement may be as much a murderer as the highwayman with knife or gun. Failing to report contagious disease is a social crime which may affect a hundred homes. An unsanitary district in the slums may start the contagion which sweeps through the city. To a crime-breeding section, left to itself, may be traced murder, arson and a hundred crimes committed on the boulevards and avenues. So in a sanitary way no man liveth to himself. Our complex civilization makes it absolutely necessary to clean up the tenements, to watch the sewerage, and to fight contagion in every part of the city, for with social beings such as we are, so long as disease lurks anywhere, no family is exempt from danger. To the altruistic citizen this argument is not necessary, for there is an inward impulse impelling him to safeguard the life of every human—even though that one may be foreign born or a pauper. Students of industrial questions are forced to give attention to accidents and disease. A great mass of the paupers and of the miserable poor have been brought to their condition through these causes rather than through lack of work, and have been compelled to live on a wage which makes it impossible for them to care properly for a family. Sickness and accidents mean a bill at the grocery, rent in arrears, less clothing, poorer food, and less power to resist disease. Oftentimes accidents mean a lowering of efficiency and consequent decrease in wage. Accidental death or crippling of the breadwinner is apt to result in the necessity of moving to poorer quarters, amid filthier surroundings, and the laying of heavy burdens upon the helpless ones when they are least able to bear them. Much of the disease among the poor is social in its origin, and for that reason society is responsible for its continuance. I have seen children dying by the score in filthy tenements, because the avaracious owner would not make the repairs needed in the toilets and sewers. Greed for the dollar is responsible for increased death rates. The city officials can materially lower the death rate in any city if they choose to do so. As science has pointed out the cause and the cure of many diseases, the officials have both the knowledge and the power to apply that knowledge. I would rather spend my time in arousing the officials to do their duty than to be content with simply comforting the broken-hearted one sitting by the bedside or bier; for while it is good to comfort, it is better to arouse to duty, if that awakening shall lessen the number of those saddened by preventable causes.

As a city grows in size and population, the individual has less and less control over the causes of disease. No longer can he obtain water from a well or spring, but must take what comes to him, even though it be contaminated at its source. Not having built his own house, he knows nothing of the plumbing or sewer connections and therefore is unable to check in time the flow of sewer gas which kills his child. He is powerless to cleanse the neglected streets or alleys which prove breeding spots for disease. And because the individual is almost helpless under existing conditions, the burden of checking disease rests the heavier upon society itself. The two things needed are rigid sanitary laws and fully instructed sanitary officials, enforcing these laws without fear or favor. To bring about these

THE CHILDREN'S HOSPITAL

things, the social conscience must be aroused
and every man led to feel that he is his brother's keeper. The war is on against unnecessary disease and death, and there is a call for
volunteers. And it pays to enforce sanitary
laws. Robert Hunter in his work entitled
"Poverty," says that the Health Department of
New York City was able during 1903 to reduce the death rate from 20 to 18.71, thus saving 4,500 lives and preventing 10,000 cases of
severe illness. "It saved the work of one or
two hospitals. It saved some wives from being widows, and some children from being
fatherless, and it also saved some from poverty." It pays to prevent disease and death.
In this City of the Angels, although growing
as a giant grows, there is hope that in time
unnecessary disease and death may be eliminated.

There is in this city an aroused social conscience. City officials as well as social workers are seeking accurate knowledge as to local
conditions, and are closely watching the results
of experiments in other cities. The housing
commission is striving for better sanitary laws.
There is a strong sentiment against ever allowing a tenement district to be established, the
preference being to scatter the population over
miles of open country now traversed by trolley
lines. The school and district nurses now report promptly all cases of contagious disease,
and being able to suggest sanitary methods of

living to the poor, are often able to save some member of the family from a protracted illness. Every city could well afford to employ a corps of district nurses as an aid to their Health Department.

The water from the nearby mountains has always been guarded so that rich and poor alike need have no fear of contamination. When the great Owens River comes rushing down from the high Sierras, it will mean health and happiness to the multitude in these sunkissed valleys.

Notwithstanding the fact that thousands of invalids seek this far-famed climate, and in many instances reach here too late, we have the remarkably low death rate of 14.96 in 1000. When a better system has been devised for handling the tuberculosis patients arriving from the East, the death rate here should be lower than it is in any other city of its size. Here the best of all remedies, fresh air and sunshine, exist in abundance. Every one in this genial climate is tempted to sleep out of doors. The tendency to do so is growing and many of the houses are built with open-air bedrooms or with large airy rooms where the windows are never closed. While this way of sleeping is just as beneficial to the health in the North and East as it is here, in this Southland it is so easy and natural that an invalid can easily be persuaded to adopt it.

The success of the treatment of New York's

bed-ridden children at Sea Breeze on Coney Island has proved the value of the fresh-air treatment for non-pulmonary tuberculosis. Hundreds of children with surgical tuberculosis, who might have become hunchbacks or cripples, are made well and strong simply by living in the open air and by breathing the salt sea air. From the same treatment, identical results would obtain on the Pacific shore that obtain on the Atlantic. When the need for such an institution becomes evident, the little sufferers of the whole Southwest will no doubt find health and strength on one of the many beaches of the greater city. As a change of climate is the best, and sometimes the only cure for asthma, what a blessing it would be for the thousands of the poor who are afflicted with this harassing disease if some philanthropist would aid them in seeking a new clime, and thus finding health and ability to make their own livelihood.

Los Angeles has become an educational center for the spread of the gospel of "a life in the open air as the only proper mode of life for human beings." This means more life out of doors; it means more windows kept open summer and winter alike. Through investigation, Robert Hunter has recently discovered that the number of breakfastless children attending school in New York amounts to many thousands. But the large majority of these did not care to eat after spending the night in a stuffy

room, that left them without any appetite for
food.

Of all the diseases that affect mankind, there
is none which is the cause of more economic
and social distresss and waste than tuberculosis—"the great white plague." Once there was
the Great Black Plague which in a few years
carried away, from two to three million people
from the cities of Europe, after which it dis-
appeared from the face of the earth. But the
great white plague has continued through the
centuries, its annual slaughter of over a million souls each year. That means that every
day of the year, 3,000 fall as its victims. Unless there shall be a decided change for the
better, 8,000,000 of the population now living
in the United States will die from consumption.
That this fearful loss of life can be checked is
the firm belief of medical scientists. It is their
confident hope that the time will come when
the daily battle now begun will at last destroy
the disease. Among the methods now employed are the dissemination of scientific
knowledge regarding the character of tuberculosis and the proper care of the patients in the
home, so that others may not contract the
disease; the treatment in properly equipped
sanitaria of those who are in its first and second stages; and the building of comfortable
hospitals for all hopeless cases, thus preventing
the possibility of further spread of disease
from those in its worst stage. In these direc-

tions great progress has already been made, and much has been done both in saving life and in checking contagion. Consumption is a house-bred disease. The dreaded germs expelled from the lungs are quickly destroyed in the sunlight, but in a dark room they may remain active for years. The history. of "the lung blocks" in our great cities is a proof of this statement. In rooms where tuberculosis patients have died, for years afterwards some member of nearly every family occupying these quarters becomes a victim of consumption. Sweatshops where diseased workmen in coughing, saturate the clothing with germs, not only spread contagion to all who become purchasers of sweatshop garments, but are made disease centers for other workmen who follow them. What a burden is laid upon the Health Departments of our cities in seeing that every room where a consumptive has lived and died has been properly fumigated, and in guarding the public from contagion in workshop and factory. To this end there should be a report made to the Health Office of every patient thus affected. There are those who believe that the time is coming when every advanced case will be segregated in a city hospital, as is now done in the case of small pox.

There are many agencies, both private and public, which are educating the general public as to the most hygienic way of caring for the patients in the home. Instruction is being given how to prevent contagion from the sputa; the kind and value of food for the sick ones; the absolute necessity for baths and fresh air; the need of keeping in mind the fact that unaffected ones must be guarded from contagion. Private philanthropy has done much towards blotting out the disease, by building sanitoria for those who are curable. These sanitoria are to be found in Canada and among the mountains of New England as well as in Colorado and California. Tents, shacks and open-air bungalows are better, however, than the more closely built hospitals. Proper food and rest are necessary, but fresh air is the best medicine, and this can be taken advantage of just as successfully at forty degrees below zero as when warmed by the southern sun.

Some years ago Mr. N. O. Nelson, a well-known philanthropist of St. Louis, established a health camp at Indio, in the Colorado desert of Southern California, where consumptives could live out of doors the year round. The charge for board is reasonable, and as Nature is the only physician, there are no added charges for doctors or medicines. There are from seventy to a hundred patients here each year, their stay averaging sixty-six days, which is a higher ratio than that of the average consumptive sanitarium. There is here a lower death rate than elsewhere, it being one in ten. Were it not for the rather excessive heat of summer, the stay would be much longer, and many

more would obtain an absolute cure in this
desert air, which is very dry, yet upbuilding in
its effects.

Dr. W. Jarvis Barlow has established a sanitarium in the foothills near Los Angeles.
This institution is located on a twenty-five-
acre tract, in a little valley in the Chavez Ravine, just to the south, and bordering on Elysian Park. It receives indigent consumptive
patients on payment of $5.00 per week, meet-
ing the extra cost by donations from the gen-
erous public. Owing to its crowded condition, the County Hospital is only able to ad-
mit tuberculosis patients in advanced or bed-
ridden stages of the disease, so the Barlow
Sanitarium is the only institution in Los Angeles which receives indigent consumptives in
the early stages of the disease, and strives to
effect a cure through the open-air treatment.
When it is borne in mind that from 25 to 50
per cent of all tuberculosis morbidity in Los
Angeles is among indigent residents, the necessity for such an institution is very appar-
ent.

There is great need, however, that these
private efforts be supplemented by institutions
maintained by the city and state. In the last
report of the Los Angeles Health Department
is found the following practical suggestion:
"If the county and city would provide suitable
sanitaria in the foothills for the care of indigent tuberculosis patients, many of the in-

cipient cases would recover and those in the advanced stage of the disease could be better cared for without injury to the non-infected." No doubt this wise suggestion will in the near future be carried out. A private organization known as the Anti-tuberculosis League has recently taken a forward step in the establishment of a "Helping Station" for the poor consumptives at the Medical College on Buena Vista Street. Dr. F. M. Pottenger, the organizer of the League, describes the work as follows: "Los Angeles has finally taken a definite step to do the right thing in preventing the spread of tuberculosis. Somewhat after the method used in Berlin, the Anti-tuberculosis League of Southern California has organized a helping station. The purpose of this helping station is not only to help those who are suffering from tuberculosis, but also to help the community at large. Tuberculosis, as is well known, is most common among the poor. It thrives in dark unsanitary quarters, and is especially found among those who are poorly fed, overworked and reduced by excess of various kinds. This helping station shall be a place where the worthy poor may come and receive treatment and instruction from competent physicians. Every patient is shown how to prevent the spread of disease. Nurses are connected with the station, who go to the house or quarters occupied by the patients and instruct them just as thoroughly as possible

BARLOW TUBERCULOSIS SANATORIUM

how they can best arrange their rooms and homes for the care of this disease. They also see the family, telling them that the danger of tuberculosis is in the expectoration, and giving them thorough instructions how to destroy this. The necessary spit cups and disinfectants are furnished by the helping station. Many of these patients suffering from tuberculosis, even if they cannot get well, can be restored to usefulness, so that they may be able to work and to support their families for several months, if they only can have the proper care and food. It is the policy of the helping station to furnish such food as milk and eggs to the needy and thus afford them the best opportunity for rapid improvement. Another important feature is the inquiry into the health of the other members of the family. Where a patient is found in a family, all its different members will be requested to go to the institution for examination. In Berlin, where this plan is carefully carried out, as many as seven persons have been found in one family suffering from the "great white plague." By taking the precaution of examining all members, the disease will be discovered early in many cases and they can be put under the proper conditions to get well.

"It is unnecessary for patients suffering from incipient tuberculosis to die. A large percentage of them can get well if treated properly; but to give them the best chance for

11

getting well the disease must be discovered early. When this is done and the patient is made aware of its presence and instructed how to care for his expectoration, almost the only source for spreading the disease has been removed.

In addition to the local work, a settlement has been established at Redlands, and plans have been laid for the creation of another health camp in the foothills near Pasadena.

The California Club is at this time working for the passage of a law making it possible to establish a state sanitarium for the treatment of tuberculosis, thus placing the possibility of a cure within the reach of every afflicted one in the state, as has already been done in several Eastern commonwealths.

The question arises as to whether California ought to bear the burden of the large number of indigent Eastern patients who come here for the climate or as a last resort. Does California offer a surer cure than can be found in the Eastern States? Dr. Woods Hutchison, physician at the Arrowhead Sanitarium, gives the following advice as to the value of climate in the treatment of patients. "To put it briefly, I believe that climate is of little importance in the treatment of tuberculosis, inasmuch as the disease can be cured in apparently as large percentage of cases and as promptly in northern and eastern climates as in any of the so-called health resorts, provided that the open-air treatment is rigidly carried out. Fresh air properly and thoroughly applied will cure tuberculosis in any known climate. I have personally seen just as satisfactory results in the suburbs of London, in the Adirondacks, in Illinois, in Iowa and in Western Oregon as in California or in Arizona. The only value of climate in the treatment of the disease is that a mild sunshiny climate makes the open-air cure easier and more pleasant to take—sugar-coats the pill, as it were. If the patient be compelled to take the open-air treatment whether he like it or not, he will recover in any climate. I am also inclined to think that patients who are cured in a northern or eastern climate are decidedly less liable to relapse than those returning to their climate after a cure effected in the South. The mass of tuberculosis patients should be treated in or near their homes, and the southern and southwestern climates used only as a luxury for those who can afford them." On the other hand, there are prominent physicians who claim that away from the coast, the hillsides, with their dry, balmy air, offer ideal places for those who can live without work.

Dr. George H. Kress, an eminent physician of Los Angeles and a thorough student of this disease, may be quoted as an authority. He says: "Belief in the specific therapeutic value of certain climates is still held not only by a large mass of laymen, but also

by a goodly proportion of medical practition-
ers. The real truth of the matter is this: There
is no such thing as a specific climate in tuberculosis. Patients suffering from that disease
get well in all kinds of climates, only of course,
certain climates possess far greater advantages than others. It is not so much a question of what climate, but how a climate is
used that is of the first importance. Southern
California, for instance, owes its advantages in
the treatment of this disease to a well-drained
soil, to the pure air coming from the deserts
and ocean, to the large number of days on
which the sun shines, and to a diurnal tem-
perature variation which, while equitable from
day to day the year round, varies sufficiently
to not be enervating, so that a tonic outdoor
life may be constantly led."

Los Angeles has also an association of benevolent individuals working toward a saner
treatment of epileptics. Hitherto epilepsy has
been regarded as almost incurable. In California these unfortunates are found in prisons,
reformatories, asylums, homes for the feeble-
minded or in their own homes. A few of the
states have adopted the colony idea, where on
the farm with good, fresh air and an opportunity to work without danger, they have a
better chance for recovery. In the Craig
Colony at Sonyea, New York, 1200 of New
York's epileptics are living on a 2000-acre
farm, helping largely in their own support.

Seven per cent of the chronic cases are returned to their homes as cured. If incipient cases were included, a much larger percentage of cure would result. Those who are especially interested in the study of this disease believe that epilepsy will soon be numbered among the curable diseases. As soon as sufficient money can be raised, it is the purpose of the Los Angeles association to secure a ranch and establish under expert management a colony for epileptics which will be a place for the study of causes and methods of cure, as well as for the treatment of patients. It is surely a sign of the increase of the altruistic spirit when so much attention is given to the treatment of diseases once considered incurable. The self-sacrifice of physicians and laymen in seeking to help a class of unfortunates, too long neglected, is worthy of as great honor as that shown to the heroes of war.

Owing to the fame of our California climate, a large number of invalids come hither every year seeking health. To meet the demand of the many well-to-do patients, a number of magnificent hospitals have been erected in Los Angeles, thoroughly scientific and up-to-date. Yet in all these hospitals there are but few free beds. There is one notable exception—the Children's Hospital on Alpine Street. Here in their own building, a large number of ladies are seeking to make it possible that every suffering child who cannot receive proper treatment at home, may have the best of care and be nursed back again to perfect health. A nurse from this place also visits sick children in their homes, thus extending more widely this blessed ministry to God's little ones.

What private philanthropy has not done for the indigent sufferer of this Southland, the city and county are doing, and are doing well. The climate which draws the rich from the colder regions also attracts the poor. Among the latter are many sick ones who have sold all they have in order to purchase a ticket to California. Hence a large number of the inmates of the County Hospital are newcomers. In the hospitals here, as in all other city and county hospitals, besides the self-respecting poor there are to be found the stranded wrecks of humanity—the scarlet woman ending her life of suffering, the wretched syphilitic and inebriate cases reaping the harvest of wild oats sown in youth.

The reform of the city poor-house is a subject which is attracting the attention of all social workers. The old work-house system with its obvious evils is gradually giving way to modern methods. The Los Angeles County Farm occupies a beautiful site, with orange and pepper, banana and palm trees, and the choicest flowers. There aged men and women can walk daily in the midst of a landscape such as money cannot buy in the East during winter. An out-of-door life in Southern California means comfort for aged poor. No land offers a better place in which to grow old, for here there are no extremes of heat and cold and the many sunshiny days make life a delight. The Soldier's Home near the city furnishes an example of how the worn-out soldier may have the best that nature affords. From the large airy buildings beautiful vista effects are to be had in every direction, and long lines of rarest trees and semi-tropical plants are bordered by great stretches of velvety lawn. Hundreds of the old soldiers are there ending their days among beauties of nature rarely equaled elsewhere.

To few do the following words of Longfellow more aptly apply than to the fortunate ones who are members of the Hollenbeck Home for the aged on Boyle Heights:

"The night hath not come yet; we are not quite
Cut off from labor by the falling light;
Something remains for us to do or dare,
Even the oldest tree some fruit may bear,
For age is opportunity, no less,
No less than youth itself, though in another dress,
And as the evening twilight fades away
The sky is filled with stars invisible by day."

Because of the entrance fee of $300, and the care taken in the selection of those who are to enter, there are gathered here a group of cultured and refined men and women in the midst of comfort and surrounded by grounds fit for a king's palace. The view from the Home extends from the snow-capped mountains almost to the sea. Growing old in California is not something to be feared. After a strenuous life one may have here a time of the greatest enjoyment.

Full well have the Catholic Sisterhoods labored with untiring zeal and self-sacrifice for the orphans, the wayward girls, and the aged poor. The Sisters of Mercy and the Little Sisters of the Poor have recently secured commodious buildings where they will carry on a work like that of the good Shepherd Himself. The followers of Frederick Ozanam in the Conference of St. Vincent de Paul are in a quiet way reaching hundreds of the poor and aged, and bringing them comfort and consolation in their homes.

We cannot close this chapter on seeking health without a word concerning the mental attitude which ought to be maintained. The fear of sickness and death has brought many a man to realize "that which I feared has come upon me." The fear of contagion creates a soil prepared for the propagation of disease germs. Every plague has its thousands of fear victims. A man may become practically immune by banishing fear, living a clean life, a normal life of loving service. By talking health and thinking health we may become

A HILL-TOP HOTEL

benefactors to our race.   Certainly in seeking health and happiness for ourselves and others, we will have no small part in making this a better city.

CHAPTER IX.

THE NON-PARTISAN

The modern city is not a model city. The simple life of our forefathers has become complex. The social, economic, and even the religious life have been changed by the incoming of a new industrial life. The popular town meeting has been replaced by the boss-ruled party caucus. Were it not for the dreamers and seers who prophesy a better city for the future, the outlook would be not only sad, but serious. A few years ago, a small group of social thinkers had visions of a new social democracy and they began at once making history, believing that a vision is the spiritual forecast of God's higher plan for mankind.

To the student of sociology there is no more significant chapter than that which describes the downward course of the city in the years following the Civil War, when a few men began to amass large fortunes, importing cheap labor and exploiting the working class in their own interest. It was then that the tenement house and the slum seemed necessities, the public not realizing that to sow a slum meant to reap an epidemic. Then it was that politics became so corrupt that an honest man did not care to run for office, and an oligarchy of misrule was established in all of our cities.

Looked at from our present-day standpoint, the intense individualism of a few decades ago seemed to produce results which were devoid of either social or ethical value. Yet the forces of righteousness were powerful and extensive. Great revivals of religion swept through the cities; mighty philanthropies were established by private initiative. One has only to read such a book as "The Better New York,"* describing the humanitarian efforts of that great city, to realize the extent to which large-hearted men and women have given themselves in service for their fellow men. Filled with altruistic zeal, many were the noble souls who devoted themselves to rescue work and deeds of charity. Most of the movements at this time were individualistic rather than social, saving a few out of the wreck, rather than charting the channel. The first great step forward consisted in organizing charity to prevent waste, and in beginning the study of the causes of poverty. During this time politics were degenerating. "To the victors belong the spoil," was the motto adopted, and well it was lived up to. Partyism was placed

---

*"The Better New York," published by the Baker & Taylor Co., of New York. It suggested the title of this volume, "The Better City."

before patriotism, resulting in graft and misrule in every great city in the land. But the day was darkest just before dawn. A few brave souls, catching the spirit of Andrew Toynbee, sought residence in the most congested parts of the great cities, to do their part in the work of social reconstruction. The story of the great achievements of social settlements and institutional churches is familiar to all. With the social conscience once aroused, it was seen that it was not enough simply to save this group or that neighborhood, but that efforts must be put forth to check the forces of evil which were in power in every great city. Agitation, resulting in sporadic attempts to drive the rascals out of office followed. The work for civic betterment at length began to take form in the organization of Civic Associations. Far reaching in their helpfulness in social uplift, the American Civic Associations had as their aim "to make cities and towns and villages clean, healthful and attractive places in which to live; to extend the making of parks in all communities; to promote the work of making playgrounds for the children and recreation centers for adults; to abate public nuisances—such as objectionable advertising signs, unnecessary electric poles and wires, and unpleasant and wasteful smoking factory chimneys; to make railway stations and factories and the grounds surrounding them tidy and ornamental; to preserve existing trees and encourage intelligent tree planting." Great as was this movement, it did not quite reach the sources of the evil affecting city life. Jacob Riis' ten years' war to cleanse the slum was to be duplicated by as vigorous an effort to cleanse the city hall.

Progress toward the better city is being surely though slowly made. The various reform movements which were quite distinct at their inception, soon merged into one another, inasmuch as it was usually the same group of men with large ideas which organized the newer and more inclusive movements. The great philanthropists of an earlier age gave themselves in an earnest effort for individual and group redemption. Charity had become organized for the first time, the great host of charity workers forming a clearing house that business principles might be applied to the handling of the vast sums of money entrusted to them. At the same time they introduced the friendly visitor, who furnished the human touch to the otherwise colder work of officialism. "To make for the social good is her one desire. To preach the social good is her one message" is written of Jane Addams, who is the best type of the worker in the great movement for social regeneration. This class of workers do not bend down to a lower group; they do not study their neighbors as specimens in a museum; but contrarywise, living their lives in a new environment; having something to give and much to receive; dealing with those around them just as "folks," every one of them capable of contributing something to the good of all. As a non-Christian land can never become Christian except by the coöperation and leadership of the natives of that land, so in city life, the better day will come only when those whom we sometimes call the common people are inspired to coöperate with their leaders in striving after the higher civic ideals. The social worker is an inspirer. The man that does the thing worth doing may come from the lower strata of society. The great mass of working men are beginning to think, and this will finally result in the overthrow of social and economic evils.

Considering that life is more than meat, and that health and happiness are the birthright of every man, the people call loudly for civic betterment and the City Beautiful. That call is answered by such men as Charles Zueblin, Daniel H. Burnham and Charles M. Robinson. It is answered by the birth of a new social spirit. After years of bitter competition in the amassing of fortunes, the coöperative movement is at last taking form. After years of graft, the altruistic spirit is manifesting itself. After individual struggle for supremacy in trade and politics, we behold ever-enlarging groups of citizens at work in making the modern city better than the vision of the best a hundred years ago. The world is growing better. No man can be a pessimist who realizes something of the spirit of the times. A local editor puts it thus tersely in these words: "Every today is a good day. Every tomorrow will be a better day to the man whose nature is sound and hopeful. Mankind advances as the tides of the ocean. Waves of advancement sweep up the beach of time, each a little higher, but each meantime receding to gain a greater impetus. When the country seems stagnant or retrograding, it is only gathering for a wider wave sweep of progress." It was said of Mayor Jones of Toledo, the "man of the Golden Rule," that he made citizenship religious. He himself became a humanizing influence, the common denominator between all classes. There are men today who love their city, and work for it just as zealously and religiously as those who gave their lives as missionaries to the cannibal islands.

As never before, the call is for men; for unlettered laborers as well as for university graduates; for men who can free themselves from the power of the trusts and the party boss; for men who are not afraid of democracy; for men who are awake to the evils of turning over the city government to the great corporations such as the railroads, the street car companies, and the breweries; for men who can gird themselves to struggle for the redemption of the city from the grasp of these

alien powers, that they may give it back again
to the people; for men who realize that there
is no necessary connection between national
policies and city government, and that the
party caucus, primary and convention, with
prearranged programs spell bondage rather
than freedom; for men who will champion the
rights of the average citizen, and will demand
clean hands in city government, and who instead
of saying, "my party right or wrong" will rather
say, "the best interests of my city, first and
last and all the time."

While not the first city to declare itself for
complete nonpartisanship in city politics, the
story of the partial victory of the city of Los
Angeles may well encourage other cities to
enter upon this latest movement in social service and civic betterment with a heart of hope.
Some two years ago, largely through the initiative of the Municipal League, a strong non-
partisan school board was nominated and
elected, thus taking the city schools out of
politics. Under the new charter the Water
Board and the Board of Public Works were
removed from politics, and both boards were
filled by some of the ablest and strongest business men of the city. Public opinion is now
so strong in this city that no mayor or council
would dare to appoint a corrupt or incompe-
tent man on either board. About one year
ago, a group of young business and professional men, mostly college men, began the

THE POLYTECHNIC HIGH SCHOOL, LOS ANGELES

movement for the nomination of a non-partisan ticket, and last July the Committee of One Hundred was organized, composed of strong and influential men. This committee through a strong executive committee began at once the selection of candidates. Meeting almost nightly for weeks and even months, they discussed name after name for every office, not asking who wanted a particular office, but who was best fitted to perform its duties. They searched the city through and through, asking advice of every one, probing the character, and looking into the history of every available candidate. How different this way from the customary method of forming a slate in the back room of a saloon! They completed their work before the party conventions convened, with the result that they succeeded in placing some of the non-partisans on the party tickets. On December 4, sixteen out of twenty-three non-partisans were elected.

The campaign was strenuous and some of the newspapers did valiant work for the cause of freedom. From the first the committee avoided personalities and the adoption of ordinary political methods, conducting rather a campaign of education by pamphlet and public addresses. Hundreds of strong speeches were delivered in halls and factories and in open air. Their manifestos were prefaced by words of leaders in American politics, like the following from President Roosevelt: "The worst

12

evils that can affect our local government arise from, and are the inevitable result of, the mixing up of city affairs with party politics of the state and nation. The lines upon which national parties divide have no necessary connection with the business of a city. Such connection opens the way to countless schemes of public plunder and civic corruption." Again in the words of Robert M. La Follette: "The intelligent and patriotic citizen will no longer allow himself to be played as a pawn in party politics to enrich the grafter. Party politics should have no place in a conflict with those who assail the life principles of our government. Before all things else, the honest voter —Republican or Democrat—must hold priceless this vital principle: the public official must faithfully represent the citizen."

The expressions of opinion of many interested in the campaign were significant, and as this was the initial campaign in this city for the breaking down of party power, and the beginning of the movement in the country at large, their utterances are worth remembering. A local judge wrote: "The city of Los Angeles is today truly a modern city, with a twentieth century charter and a twentieth century ambition. Her affairs are the affairs of a big corporation. Her business cannot be managed by little minds. Merely to maintain cleanliness and order in such a city requires a high order of fidelity and ability. The politi-

cal affairs of a city are not the affairs of a
political national party. While parties in city
government may and will exist, they must become purely municipal parties if they are to
be beneficial to the city."

"An independent movement of citizens to
elect city officers is not an anti-party movement. It is just a step toward municipal party
organization. It means that the citizens have
some initiative force, and intend to apply that
force where it will do some good."

"I believe that in the not far distant future,
municipal parties will regularly exist for the
settlement of municipal policies, and for the
election of officers to administer them; that in
those days party nominations will be made by
direct vote of the people; that conventions will
be restricted to their proper functions of de-
claring party principles, and promoting the
success of those measures to which the party
has committed itself. Under those conditions
a city will not have any boss office distributor.
Its bosses will be men whom the people have
chosen, and not those who have chosen themselves to rule over the people."

A well-known capitalist puts the matter
thus: The non-partisan movement is a good
one. The situation demands it. It is sane and
in harmony with the best interests of the city.
In older communities representative men, well
qualified for such work are often willing to
take upon themselves civic responsibilities and

often there are enough of these in either party to secure a reasonably safe administration. But in this city where the business situation is tense, where each year's development exceeds the expectations of the most enthusiastic and where men are giving attention only to their personal business there comes the chance for political manipulation.

"Under the guise of party the most unstable men are pushed into high offices—men whose previous business experience or mental stamina renders them totally unfit for office. Something that will take the management of city affairs out of the hands of men of small calibre and the bosses, is demanded.

"Our city affairs are now of such proportions, and the funds handled are so tremendously large, and the business interests are so critical that none but the best men, morally and from the standpoint of business ability, should be put in power. Experience tells that we cannot get that class of men from our party machines.

"The non-partisan movement, it is evident, is not in the interests of any clique or individual, but for the general public welfare. It should command the careful thought and hearty coöperation of all citizens."

A clergyman offered the following ethical argument: "A new spirit is in the air. It is the altruistic and the practical. As there is always a man behind every great institution, so there will be a man or men behind this new movement, strongly dominated by the spirit of civic righteousness. The members of the Committee of One Hundred are evidently the men for the occasion. They are largely young men who have never been connected with the machine, but are willing in an unselfish way to work for the public good.

"Our best citizens have been busy in making money, in building up professional reputations, in using their leisure for merely personal recreation. Many of the idle rich are seeking everywhere for some new form of pleasure, and do not realize that he who serves his fellow men is the one to whom comes the greatest pleasure. This is what makes life worth the living.

"There is something better than mere money making; better than the making of a great reputation; better than the mere killing of time. It is found in social service—talents used for the good of all; spare time used for the social uplift; earnest thought devoted to the changing of evil conditions and bad environment; ability along commercial lines freely given in solving the financial problems of a great city. There is a rising tide of brotherly kindness, and this reveals itself in something more than charity. The world needs not the dole for today, but more real love between man and man. It is a sign of the times that we find some of the best people of our land interested in Ward Improvement Associations; housing committees; in planning practical temperance movements, offering substitutes for the saloon; in law enforcement; in exploiting graft; in social settlement work; in the study of municipal ownership and coöperative schemes. It is safe to say that the members of the Committee of One Hundred belong to this class."

A leading banker, strong in his advocacy of the new movement, says: "Purity in politics does not, as I understand it, express the full extent and scope of the new non-partisan movement. In its truest and most complete sense, the movement means the election to office of men whose worth has been established in the business world, who have proven by the management of their own affairs their fitness to govern those of the municipality.

"Ability should be added to purity in the demands of the non-partisan party. It should demand that the men who accept office should have an understanding of the vast and vital interests they will be called upon to influence after their election. A politician may be ever so honest and clean in the commonplace acceptance of the term, but he should have other qualifications than that of merely having proved useful to his party or political superior when he is placed in a position of trust in a city like Los Angeles, with its millions of invested money and great business enterprises.

"I am not attacking anyone, but I feel that the city is entitled to the best material it can get. I feel that the man in office should at least have as much business experience as the man who has managed some private enterprise and managed it successfully. Such a man would not only be pure, in the acceptance of the term as applied to the present movement, but should be competent.

"The following is from a well-known educator: Prominent men of high standing will not run for municipal office upon party tickets. We have plenty of good men who would have the complete confidence and almost unanimous support of citizens if they should consent to become candidates, but they refuse to descend into the muck of machine politics. This is one of the reasons why party lines should be done away with locally. Chosen by the people and promised the support as citizens' candidates, clean business men will be found to take up these burdens as duties.

"The non-partisan movement is the solution. Los Angeles sadly needs men of good principle, of known integrity; men with rigid spinal columns and business ability to administer her affairs in the cause of good government. I have talked with many such men and all declare that they could not be induced to enter the way of deceit, lies, and mud slinging into which machine candidates are plunged from the very start. But these same men of honor can be induced to run through a clean movement of non-partisan character. I believe that we are going to see noble men who have the respect of the entire city put into office."

The following quotation is taken from the declaration of a retired capitalist: "The day of ringsters is passed. The people have arisen and declared that they will be independent in their voting, putting into office the candidates of their choice. The whole people never will go wrong on a proposition of this character. Now that they are doing their own thinking, their own nominating, and their own voting, the very best type of men will be put into office.

"The non-partisan spirit is gaining force throughout the country daily. The movement for a general clean-up along political lines is gaining and the people themselves are going to see that the anti-political remedy is administered in large doses. Experience has proved to my satisfaction that politics in municipal affairs is a detriment to good government and should not be tolerated for a moment. I believe that Los Angeles is going to rise above party lines and I expect to see the city advance rapidly under a business administration."

To the same effect are the words of a prominent attorney: "The awakening of the people all over the country to corruption in public

OLD SPANISH OLIVE MILL

affairs is an encouraging thing in our political life. We see that our form of government in which each individual is accorded equal rights, is controlled by public opinion, instead of being controlled by a few minds as is usually the case in other forms of government. This public sentiment is irresistible in its power. It is this power which has throttled the trusts in tobacco, paper, gunpowder and fertilizers, and has convicted the meat packers, and made the great railroad corporations yield in their rebates.

"The same powerful force during the last few years has lifted our city from much of the grafting of the past and is educating public sentiment here so that we may have better service, better work for the expenditures and a much improved civic tone. The independent citizen is directly responsible for this improvement. Party lines can no longer hold the independent and intelligent voters to party tickets in local affairs."

The campaign of 1906 is ended. The people have spoken, but the real work has just begun. The Committee of One Hundred has not disbanded, but is more active than ever in a campaign of education. Three years more of this leadership and the politicians of this city will not dare to stand for else than the broad principle of non-partisanship in municipal affairs.

In social settlement, in church, in club, and

on the platform, the theme which awakens the greatest enthusiasm today is that of the Better City. But the vision must become the reality. Hitherto we have abdicated as sovereign citizens in favor of self-appointed bosses, content to vote for the party nominee, regardless of his character. "I once thought," said a young Italian voter during the last campaign, "that all there was to an election was the casting of your vote. Now I know that politics is a great study." By this he meant that to secure the largest number of votes for his party, that he might be in on the larger graft, required careful scheming and shrewdness. Politics is indeed a "study," but it should be a study in ethics.

The world persists in calling every effort for reform and for the establishment of civic righteousness, a campaign or a war. Rather let us look upon it as the spiritual conception of history; the recognition of the non-material forces at work for human betterment; the power of ideals; the bringing to pass of the vision of the few; the self-sacrifice of noble souls; the operation of unseen divine forces that create new conditions. No one can claim to be the originator of these modern movements. He who leads is the one who has come into the most perfect harmony with the spirit of the times; the one who feels the mighty uplift of the unseen forces, and who seeks to draw others into the same noble serv-

ice. God and right are no more on the side of
the strongest machines than they are on the
side of the strongest battalions. Think, my
fellow citizen, on those things that make for
the better city; join hands with others of like
mind who are laboring for the common weal;
rejoice in what has already been accomplished;
be pure and lofty in purpose, persistent in
effort, and remember that a few can lead a
multitude.

There are many helpful methods that have
been tried or suggested for securing better
city government. A change for the better can
be made by the elimination of the voting circle
at the head of the party ticket; and better still,
the elimination of the party ticket itself, and
the substitution of an arrangement requiring a
mark for every candidate voted on; the absolute elimination of every distinguishing mark
on the ballot; a requirement making it necessary for every candidate to be nominated by
petition. The initiative and referendum, with
the recall, place the power where it belongs—
in the people's hands.

That there are still better plans to be
evolved, no one doubts. "Election by examination is the beginning of election by education,
which Emerson prophesied," says Henry De-
morest Lloyd.* A training school for city officials may become as necessary and as com-

*From Lloyd's, "Man, the Social Creator."

mon as the technical, professional or commercial schools are now. Why not have men carefully prepared in mind and morals so that the leaders of the people may be selected instead of elected? This is truly in line with the great movements for civic betterment.

The experiment of a city government by commission is now being tried with great success in Galveston and Houston, Texas. Following the great hurricane of 1900, Galveston was almost forced to adopt this system because of the chaotic condition of the city government. A mayor-president and four commissioners have full charge of all the city affairs, as a board of directors might have in any well-managed corporation. All other elective officers have been abolished and the whole responsibility is placed upon this board.

This new plan of city government has attracted the attention of many other municipalities with a result that three states have passed laws providing for commission government based on this Texas idea. Experts regard as best the modified form of commission government, which will become effective next March in Des Moines, Iowa.

"Business, not politics," is a good watchword; but "equality of opportunity" is a better one. It is the inalienable right of every man to make the best of himself; to breathe fresh air; to live in a sanitary dwelling; to be able to enjoy life in parks and on boulevards;

to have the best of schools for his children, and community centers for refinement and culture; to secure a living wage, and thus be able to secure the greatest of all blessings, a home for his family, be that home but a cottage or a bungalow. When every citizen comes to his own, and every citizen seeks the welfare of every other citizen, then we will have the Better City.

CHAPTER X.

INDUSTRIAL LIFE

"The City of the Angels," so attractive to the tourists because of climate and natural beauty, is fast becoming a great industrial center. The Panama Canal will bring the ships of the world to its own harbor. The awakening of the nations across the Pacific will create demands for goods manufactured in coast cities. Oil fuel is at hand, transportation is assured, and a vast market is being opened. Capital will quickly respond, and soon the loom and the furnace will furnish products for a new world of commerce. Already great industrial plants are busy day and night satisfying the demands of an ever-widening district.

But the growth of industrial life is always fraught with grave dangers. The industrial revolution of the past wrought also a social revolution. The days of arcadian simplicity on the ranchos and in the region around the Franciscan missions have long gone by. The call of the factory whistle is louder and more insistent than the sweet music of the mission bells. The long line of Indians on their way to the morning mass is now replaced by throngs of laborers rushing to their daily toil.

The farmer boys no longer look forward to the time when they own a ranch of their own with its wealth of orange, grape and peach— but drawn by an irresistible power, they expect to become laborers in the city shop and mill, and live in congested quarters, so different from the open life on the farm. Mastered by the social unrest of the time, they will become a part of the great army of labor fighting for industrial freedom, and will perforce have a share in the industrial and economic problems of great trade centers which now seem so far from solution. Already the conflict is upon us, and the oligarchy of capital is arraying itself against labor organized in self-defense.

As factories increase in size and number, aliens will be attracted, tenements and house courts will become congested, causing an increase of sickness and crime. Industrial accidents will cripple productive power, and thus throw heavy burdens on public charity and private philanthropy; and the customary labor of women and children in factory life will tend still further toward the deterioration of home life.

Although certain evils will necessarily follow the extension of the new industrialism, this city will not lag behind in its efforts to right the wrongs. Moved by the spirit of the times, there are many men and women who with loving heart and altruistic spirit are

studying modern problems, and are seeking to
apply their high ideals to practical life. Witness the recent non-partisan movement; the
efforts of the Park Commission to provide
parks and boulevards; the efforts of the Civic
Association to make this the City Beautiful;
the efforts of the Housing Commission to establish by law a new type of houses for congested quarters; the work of the labor union
and the socialist body in their efforts to better
conditions in the economic world. The work
of these and many other similar groups reveals the fact that the social conscience is
aroused and conditions can never again be as
bad as of old.

There are three parties interested in the solution of present-day problems of industrial life.
They are the employer, the employed and the
general public, each one of whom is more or
less selfishly interested, and all of whom are
working either blindly or intelligently for the
good of all. The division of labor in modern
factory life has made man a part of a machine,
known by number rather than by name. "The
man with a number" becomes to the master
a man without a soul, for under this method
the employer loses the touch of human interest and the sense of brotherhood, and therefore forgets entirely the spiritual significance
of the lives that are devoted to his service. A
better day is surely at hand, when employers
of labor will give more attention to the physi-

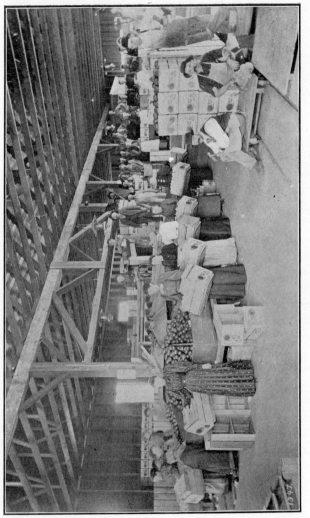

PACKING ORANGES—A CALIFORNIA INDUSTRY

cal and mental needs of their workmen. "Welfare work" this is called. Selfish, do you say? Yes, so it is often confessed to be. The work of the social secretary, in seeking the comfort and to some extent the social uplift of the employees, makes good more than her salary to her employer in the increased efficiency of the force. A recent writer in the Pacific Magazine quotes the code of the Superintendent of the Santa Re Reading Room System, as follows: "By seeking their (employees') moral, physical and financial betterment, a greater measure of contentment may be achieved, and the motive for seeking their welfare and happiness lies intimate to the success of the operation of the entire system, the perfecting of the service, the reward and encouragement of faithfulness in service. By making our men comfortable, self-reliant, by building up their aspirations, we protect our property and our business. The management recognizes that we are one family—the success of one is the success of all. We close a good deal of the gap between the high executive official and the man 'way out on the line'; we avoid disastrous changes in the service and incidentally assure our men of a life job and better conditions; by affording them actual opportunities of self-development, or bettering their education, we contribute to home making, a truer, higher civic condition, and . . . we would like to

13

have our men bound to the company by ties of regard rather than those of necessity."

This is selfish interest, perhaps selfishness. More dollars made if men are better cared for. Grant it, yet we must confess that such "welfare work" has its part in the evolution of an industrial democracy. It is at least a glimpse of the day when all men will live and labor in a clean, healthy and beautiful environment.

The following notable examples of welfare work may reveal somewhat of the plans of certain employers in their efforts to solve industrial problems. In a thorough investigation of this kind of work, Mr. Budgett Meakin* has gathered many facts regarding the efforts which have been made to lift up both socially and morally, the employees in factory and store. In speaking of the Social Secretary, he says that no firm once employing such a helper would ever dispense with the service of this assistant, for through such work "harmony has come to business, and friction and discord and discontent among employees have ceased; they see the change and feel it and the result of the system tinged with kindness and consideration for others with an atmosphere of good thoughts, has brought not only increased trade, but it makes it real pleasant to shop in these stores." The best of our great modern

---

*Model Factories and Villages.

business establishments are seeking the comfort and convenience of their patrons.

A large department store now building in Los Angeles has plans for gorgeous parlors, retiring rooms, reading and writing rooms; a nursery; an emergency hospital with physicians and trained nurses; escalators or moving stairways; a great entertainment hall; and besides a roof garden for the public. Some stores are furnishing meals at cost to their help; they are also giving sick benefits, and are maintaining schools for the cash boys. The custom of allowing pay during the summer vacations is also extending.

No modern industrial movement means more for the welfare of the working people than the transfer of manufacturing plants from the crowded city to the country, where with better housing conditions, better sanitation, fresh air, greater freedom from temptation, and with flowers and parks and bright work rooms, life seems worth the living. Chief among the factories which have set this noble example may be noted the Cadburys of England, who left Birmingham for the rural Bournville, five miles out. Their rivals, the firm of Rowntrees of York, followed their example by moving to a seventy-acre tract, building as did the Cadburys a model factory and model village. The Levers of Port Sunlight; the Clarks of Street, near Glastonbury; Messrs. Chivers of Histon, near Cambridge;

Mr. Graves of Sheffield, have all built factories in the open, where they may have plenty of light and air and flowers. Both in this coun try and in England some of the great printing houses have moved their plants to the country, and have greatly benefited their workmen. "From an aesthetic point of view, the advantages of such a removal are manifest. And we have yet to realize as a nation what an influence lovely or unlovely surroundings have on our lives and our products."

In America this movement is well under way. The Waltham Watch Works near Boston, and the Crane Paper Mills near Pittsfield, Massachusetts, are both situated on a river bank overlooking rural scenes, park-like in effect; the Natural Food Company have a palace-like factory above Niagara Falls, surrounded by park gardens, and a playground for the children; even in the city many factories are giving attention to cleanliness and beauty, by planting vines, painting work rooms in bright, cheery colors, and abating the smoke nuisance. The National Cash Register Company of Dayton, Ohio, has been able to dispose entirely of the smoke from its foundry.

The new profession of factory architect has sprung up, involving a careful study of all modern industrial problems. The Western Electrical Instrument Company is said to have employed two such experts, whose duty it was to visit factories in all parts of the United

States, studying construction and machinery;
and still a third was engaged to travel for a
year, studying welfare work of other companies.

The preservation of life and limb has never
received the attention it deserves, but public
sentiment is now demanding the introduction
of safety devices in all manufactures. Attention
is being drawn to this subject through the
establishment of museums for the display of
safety devices and appliances which have been
found serviceable. Notable progress in this
direction has been made in France and Germany. An Exposition of Safety Devices and
Industrial Hygiene, which was held in New
York in February, and the Industrial Exposition in Chicago in March, undoubtedly brought
about good results in the prevention of industrial accidents.

That ugliness, dirt and bad odors are not
necessary concomitants of factory life has
been proved by the construction and management of modern buildings where cleanliness is
maintained, and where all smoke and noxious
fumes are drawn off by exhaust fans. Many
employers are furnishing seats for their employees wherever possible and are giving attention to the elimination of nerve-racking
noises. Others are furnishing meals to their
workers at cost, sometimes even below cost,
and in many instances well-equipped dining
rooms are being built as an essential part of

the plant. Recreation is now considered necessary in the best of factories. Relaxation
from work at short intervals, with physical
culture exercises, a run out of doors, or a drill
in the gymnasium afford a change which con-
serves both health and energy. Baths, singing
and dancing classes, libraries and club rooms
add much to the enjoyment of life.

Pensions and model cottages, profit sharing
and copartnership, are more than palliative
measures; they reveal the dawning of the conviction that "man owes more to man than
wages or food or clothing or shelter." While
the familiar phrase "it pays" seems to furnish
the only incentive yet worked out in actual
life, it has its educational value both for master and man. As one writer puts it: "It pays
to treat factory people like human beings, to
insure them healthful and beautiful surroundings, and to appeal to them as possessed of a
mind and not simply of bodies. When this
potent fact has been grasped by more employers, our factory towns will not be the re-
pellant places that many of them are now, and
our factory people will not be spoken of merely
as 'hands' and very dirty ones at that."

One of the captains of industry who has advanced the farthest in social experiments is
Mr. N. O. Nelson. So wonderfully has he succeeded in introducing the coöperative principle at Leclaire, Illinois, that an extended notice of his experiment may be helpful to others.

In 1890 Village Leclaire was started. It was situated eighteen miles north of St. Louis on the highland of Illinois, adjoining Edwardsville. The purpose for which it was founded was to provide modern facilities for manufacturing, and better conditions of living. One hundred and twenty-five acres of rich, gently undulating land were secured, abutting on the station of the Toledo, St. Louis & Western Railroad. About ten acres of this were reserved for factory and public purposes, the remainder being laid out, park fashion, for residence use.

Mr. Nelson writes: "We set out to make economical healthy work shops, and to provide facilities for recreation and education other than that supplied by the public schools, to make homes for the employees with modern conveniences, and to make the place attractive in appearance. We counted on doing this by providing the proper facilities, giving the opportunity and letting the people do the rest. We started with the idea of complete individual freedom, no arbitrary authority, and have continued this policy to the present time. We named it Leclaire in recognition of the eminent services of the Parisian of that name, who first introduced profit sharing with employees.

"Starting in a wheat field without any other improvements than rail fences, and at the end of sixteen years of good and bad times this is how Leclaire now stands: Every employee

who wishes it has or may have a house in
Leclaire, buying it at the cost of construction
by our own building force, plus five per cent
for general management, paying for it and the
lot in monthly installments varying from $10
to $25 per month. The amount of monthly
payment is arranged according to what a man
can afford. If he is a foreman or a mechanic
with a large salary and a small family, he pays
larger instalments than the laboring man at a
$1.75 per day and with a large family. This, as
well as the size and style of the house and
location, is amicably arranged in advance. It
is noteworthy that no employee has ever had
any money saved up to make an advance payment, neither has any employee ever failed to
make a payment so as to cause any trouble
whatever, and there has never been a fore-
closure. A large number of homes have long
since been paid for.

"It has never been our design to confine it
to our employees; others are equally welcome
to buy lots and build for themselves. The
deeds are made in fee simple, with two pro-
tective clauses—a front building line of thirty
feet and restricting the use to residence, education or benevolent purposes. That settles
the whole question of saloon, livery stable or
other undesirable business neighbors.

"The price of lots goes to pay for public improvements. The chief streets are winding
and all paved with cinders and bordered by

HOLLENBECK HOME FOR THE AGED

trees, grass and sidewalks. The water and electric light in all the houses are supplied by the company, the price of water being $5 a year for unlimited use, and twenty-five cents a month for electric lights. If for any reason a man ceases to live in Leclaire, he is free to sell it to anyone else, or he may sell it to the company at the cost and pay rent for the time he has occupied it. The lots are from fifty to one hundred feet front, most of the early houses being built on one hundred feet, but the later ones mostly seventy-five feet. Every spring a wholesale order for fruit trees, shrubbery, plants and seeds is made up of the individual wants of the residents. Nearly all the homes are well stocked with shrubbery, fruit trees, flowers and gardens in the rear.

"There is a bowling alley, billiard room, baseball ground, an artificial lake of seven acres for boating and fishing in the summer and skating in winter. There is a hall for dancing, lectures, singing and family parties. There is no municipal organization, no mayor, police or boss. There has never been any violence or any 'drunk' or any use for an officer. The streets are lighted and sprinkled and kept in good order. The public services are attended to by the company in the same manner as its other business, theoretically acting as the representative of the residents, doing only those things which everybody wants done. The residents may at any time organize a municipality and control their own affairs. The company is well adapted to doing the work in the cheapest and best manner, and so long as it performs this duty well, there will be no occasion for change. There never has been even a suggestion of a change.

"By the average of the United States, Leclaire should have had 180 arrests during its lifetime. It has had none. It should have had a death rate of seventeen in a thousand; it has had about four. All of its children have passed through the kindergarten which has been maintained from the beginning."

Within a few years in accordance with this plan, to the employees and customers will come by the simple method of profit sharing, the full ownership of this great business. The complete success of this scheme ought to inspire many more capitalists to think of the other fellow, as well as of themselves. Mr. Nelson points out that the very living together as men produces results not otherwise obtainable. He says: "Our people are of all nationalities, drawn mainly from the cities, used to the city worker's manner of living. They have improved by no influence but themselves and their neighbors and the public facilities, such as every city and town aims and hopes to have for its well-to-do. There are no rules and regulations; no law except that of the state and county; no one is ever asked to cut his grass or keep in his chickens. Being wholly free, he and his family choose to stand as well as any of his neighbors, and fashions his home and his ways accordingly."

Every success of that like Mr. Nelson's is illuminating and inspiring, for it shows us the possibility of making men out of what seems common stuff. Says Ruskin: "We have studied and much perfected of late the great civilized invention of the great division of labor, only we have given it a false name. It is not, truly speaking, the labor that is divided, but the men—divided into mere segments of men—broken into small fragments and crumbs of life, so that all the little piece of intelligence that is left is not enough to make a pin or a nail, but exhausts itself in making the point of the pin or the head of the nail. Now it is a good and desirable thing, truly to make many pins in a day; but if we could only see with what crystal sands their points were polished —sand of a human soul, much to be magnified before it can be discerned for what it is—we should think there might be some loss in it also. And the great cry that rises from our manufacturing cities, louder than their furnace blast, is all in very deed for this: That we manufacture everything there except men; we blanch cotton and strengthen steel, and refine sugar, and shape pottery; but to brighten and strengthen, to refine or to form a single living spirit, never enters into our estimate of advantages."

In his "Christianity and the Social Problems," Dr. Lyman Abbott discusses the standard of value, concluding that the social and industrial system is to be measured not by the wealth it produces, but by the men it produces; not by the abundance of material things, but by the kind of men developed in the process. Men, not things, is the standard of value. An industrial system must produce good men or it fails. The writer by an appeal to facts, shows that our present industrial system is not giving steady and permanent employment to all willing laborers; that the system fails to give to all those employed under it wages adequate for a livelihood. If by the word "livelihood" is meant that which nourishes the mind and the spirit as well as the body, then any system that is to produce the best results must be itself educational and allow adequate leisure for the working out of educational processes. An essential condition of human well-being is a pure, good home; but to maintain a home under the present system of housing of the industrial population is well nigh impossible.

The growth of the altruistic spirit is rapidly bringing all men to believe in the statement of Tolstoi that "men think there are at times circumstances when one may deal with human beings without love, and there are no such circumstances. One may deal with things without love; one may cut down trees, make bricks, hammer iron without love, but you cannot deal with men without love." Grant this fact, and what employer would be willing to employ child labor; conduct a sweat shop; give men less than a living wage; cause them to work in unsanitary factories, or have a part in any of the multitude of evils now common in industrialism? A man is more than a machine, and because of that, a factory can be made to produce spiritual as well as material products. Not alone the idealist, but many a man of business who is a thinking man, believes in the coming of the coöperative commonwealth, in which every man shall have equality of opportunity. Edwin Markham expresses the thought of many students of the teachings of the Nazarene, when he says: "Jesus set himself to organize a social order that should shift the center of social gravity from common greed to common God; from private weal to common weal. The state was to be made the organ of love. Sublime conception! The purpose to unite the sacred with the secular, to give the spirit a working body in the world."

A modern captain of industry imbued with these high ideals, believes that men should use their abilities as well as properties for the good of all. A man owes his abilities to the public because he is a part of the whole, and would be nothing without the whole. That is implied in all talk about public spirit, public duty, public service, not to mention fellowship, brotherhood, and religion. While there are a growing number of employers interested in welfare work, and in the solution of industrial problems, it yet remains a fact that the system goes on as of yore—grinding out dollars without regard to the human element. If existing evils are not remedied by those possessing wealth, education and culture, there should be no complaint if the working class, so adversely affected by these conditions, should arise in their might and demand that to which they are entitled as men. The working men of the world have been compelled to unite. Not understanding the great principles underlying an industrial democracy, the great mass have struck and been locked out. They have suffered together in a sacrificial spirit. They have often fought over minor matters, and have committed crimes in the name of labor; yet it cannot be denied that nearly all of the improvement of the conditions under which men work has come about through the high ideals of united labor. Shorter hours of labor, increase of wages, employer's liability, the abolition of child labor, the regulation of women's work, have been fought for and partial victories have been obtained. Not alone are the unions working for better conditions, but in increasing numbers the laboring men are working in connection with the Socialist party for the coöperative commonwealth, some as idealists and some as opportunists, yet all believing that the present competitive system is doomed, and that a coöperative commonwealth is destined to take its place.

That employer and employed are interested in questions of industrial life is evident, but in these questions the general public, the great third party, is also vitally concerned. It is the public that pays the price, and from its ranks come the reformers who devote themselves with religious zeal to the solution of these industrial problems. The work of enlightenment takes place through academic discussions, magazine articles, investigations of trusts and monopolies, exhibitions in cities, which show actual conditions of factory life, thus educating public opinion and in many other ways furthering the cause of labor.

The public also pays the social price. Part of the price may consist in industrial accidents. Families and individuals are thus thrown back upon the public and fill the hospitals, asylums and almshouses; it is the public and not the employer who pays the bill. The child slave, broken in spirit, becomes a pauper, and the public pays the social price.

That all employers are not opposed to trade unions is evident from the words of the great English manufacturer, George Cadbury. He says: "My reasons for supporting trades unions are largely ethical. Without such bodies wages are brought down to the lowest point;

take for example the seamstresses of London, whose wages are only just sufficient to keep soul and body together. Only trades unions can secure collective bargaining. Without them the individual worker must be at a great disadvantage compared to the employer. They tend to high wages and thus to secure a more equal division of wealth of a country, which can only be termed truly prosperous when the bulk of its inhabitants are in comfort. England with all its colonies and wealth cannot be said to be a prosperous country while millions of its people are on the verge of starvation and living in unhealthy slums."*

No fair judgment can be passed on the action of united labor without considering carefully the reasons compelling them to action. Why is there so much unrest and discontent? Is it the result of a few paid agitators, or does it spring from a deeper cause? Consider some of the abuses against which labor presents a solid front. In the first place, let attention be paid to the conditions under which women work. Hard labor for women is not in accord with twentieth century ideals; yet it is reported that there are 130,000 women who are working in 3,900 factories in New York City, and that large numbers of them stand all day at their work; many operate dangerous machines; many work in air laden with steam and

---

*British Trade Review, January, 1898.

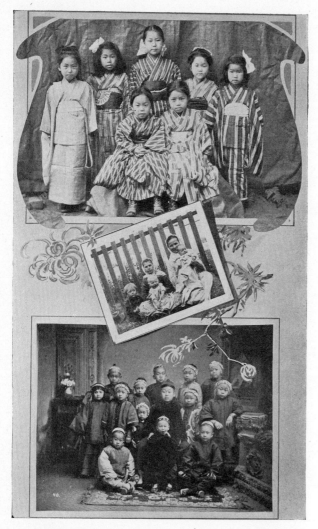

JAPANESE, RUSSIAN AND CHINESE CHILDREN

dusty fiber; some work in dark, ill-ventilated rooms, while all work under a high pressure of speed. Then there is the effort made by united labor to suppress child labor, which in this country is beginning of late to receive some measure of the attention which it deserves. Think of it! Over 1,700,000 children in the United States, under the age of sixteen, who are in the ranks of the toilers.* Does our country realize the import of these figures? But figures do not tell the story of the child taken in tender years from the influence of the home; of the little form working long hours under an intense strain which only a mature body can stand; of the physical, the mental and the moral degeneration following the lack of proper play and education and uplifting influences necessary to the normal development of youth. They do not tell of tired bodies prematurely aged; of accidents so prevalent that leave them crippled and maimed for life. They do not tell of the army of paupers, vagrants and criminals which society will have to support when the energy of the workers shall have been drained, or they have turned in disgust from a system that grinds out life and makes them at best mere soulless, automatic contrivances; nor do they tell of the dire effects upon the next generation, upon the offspring physically degenerate. The awful con-

---

*Census, 1,752,000.

14

summation of such a system is seen in England where for so long a time child labor was practiced, and where today the problem of the unemployed is pressing so heavily. Dr. Samuel M. Lindsay, Secretary of the National Child Labor Committee, who has made a thorough study of conditions in England, declares that to a large extent the unemployed are not those who will not work, but those who are unable to meet the demands of modern manufacturing life; not merely out of work, but not able to do the work required. "In brief, they are ineffectives." Already in the South a "factory" type is being developed, distinguishable by a sallowness of complexion and physical under development.

Dr. Lindsay in his article entitled, "Child Labor a National Problem," declares that, "Our standards of living, our tests of industrial efficiency, as well as our educational opportunities, have increased at a rapid rate in the last few years. So much greater is the wrong therefore that is done to the children who are deprived of even the ordinary opportunities to prepare for the greater demands of the future when they reach the years of adult life. Child labor in America means that as a nation we are deliberately breeding social inequality and striking at the roots of democracy. Ostrich fashion we only bury our heads in the sands of temporary excuses—that of industrial necessity, or the poverty of the parents, or the absurd fallacy that we are giving an industrial education to the child worker—when we refuse to look squarely in the face of the inevitable consequences of our madness and our racial folly."

Work has its part in the child's education, but the conviction is growing throughout the country today, that with the advent of machinery and modern industrial methods, child labor, not only is failing to educate, but is tending to degeneration. Against this evil of child labor are arrayed the forces of the labor unions, woman's clubs, social settlements, and many other organizations of social workers.

It is almost incredible how awful is the waste occasioned by industrial accidents. Dr. Josiah Strong contends that our peace vocations cost more lives every two days than we lost in battle during the war with Spain. The Pennsylvania coal fields furnish annually "an industrial Bull Run." And this leader in social service reminds us that men are worth more than things. "Needless slaughter is criminal slaughter. Industrial homicide is being committed every hour of the day, and the employer who does not provide every practical means for safeguarding life and limb is *particeps criminis*. Nor is the indifferent public innocent. We need to be more deeply impressed with the value and sanctity of human life. A man is worth more than the things which he

makes, or mines, or transports. To sacrifice
life to things, whose only use is to minister
to life, is perversion. It is the prostitution of
the higher to the lower.

"Suffering and death, bereavement and want
are the terrible prices paid by others that we
may enjoy the necessaries, comforts and luxuries of modern civilization. The market price
—the price which we pay—is only a part of the
actual cost. To eyes that can see, the cost
mark is written in blood—'a damned spot' that
will not 'out' so long as dividends are more
precious than human lives."*

It is a fact of history that for years the representatives of labor in this country were almost alone in their heroic struggle to bring
about the enactment of laws prohibiting or
regulating child labor, improving conditions
and shortening the hours of women's work,
enforcing the employer's liability acts, and in
bringing about the adoption of life-saving devices in factories and on railways and where-
ever labor and life were endangered by machinery. One may find fault with the methods
used in labor's struggle, yet it must be recognized that the higher ideals of real religion
and true education are impelling these toilers
to strive and to strike in order that their children may live the larger life.

What is the central issue of the labor move-

---

*Josiah Strong.

ment? Ask those who are best informed and
they will tell you that "it is nothing less than
the concerted movement of the majority of the
world's workers for recognition of human
rights and personal values in the working
world; the more or less organized effort of
fellow craftsmen and federated forces of all
trades unions to attain and maintain that
standard of life and comfort which makes it
possible for 'men to live the lives of men.' The
general movement thus described includes
such specific objects of pursuit as a living
wage, upon which depends the existence of
the home, with wifehood, motherhood and
childhood; a fairer share of leisure and privilege involving limitation of hours of labor and
the extension of the opportunities for relief
from the monotony of subdivided toil; protection of the life, limb and the health of the
working man, woman and child; a tenable social status with the possibility of peace,
progress and human brotherhood."

Los Angeles is yet to be a great manufacturing center. Will this mean industrial war between classes? Or will the vision of Andrew
Toynbee, expressed in the following words,
find fulfillment in this City of the Angels: "Let
us remember even in these moments of depres-
sion, that there never has been such a time
when such union between the classes has been
possible as it is today, or soon will become.
For not only has the law given to workmen

and employer equality of rights, but education bids fair to give them equality of culture. We are all, now, workmen as well as employers, inhabitants of a larger social world; no longer members of a single class, but fellow citizens of one great people; no longer the poor recipients of a class tradition, but heirs of a nation's history. Nay more, we are no longer citizens of a single nation—we are participators in the life of mankind, and joint heirs of a world's inheritance. Strengthened by this wider communion, and ennobled by this vaster heritage, shall we not trample under foot the passions that divide, and pass through the portals of a new age to inaugurate a new life?"

CHAPTER XI.

ORGANIZED RELIGION SOCIALIZED

Organized religion is the power making for righteousness in every community. It is powerful because religion stands for that which is highest and noblest in the development of man, and when organized, represents a mighty force for moral uplift. The Pilgrim Fathers brought with them the Church and the School, and these were the first institutions planted in every community as the frontier was pushed onward toward the Western sea. Religious zeal sent men and women to the cannibal islands, where their labors of love produced results almost miraculous. They became the teachers in the Orient, and the awakened nations now thank them for their great aid in the time of transition.

While it needs no argument to prove that much has been done by organized religion for the betterment of the world, and the ushering in of an ideal society, the world calls for better results in the future than in the past. It is the purpose of this chapter to show that the return to the original social ideals of Christianity is what is needed in the religious life of today.

Jesus the Nazarene was a spiritual teacher, and not the founder of an organization. He was a seer, with the vision of a new, God-permeated society, freed from the animalism and corruption into which man had sunk; a society which had been dimly foreseen by the prophets, who told of a day to come when "men helped everyone his neighbor, and everyone said to his neighbor, Be of good courage." He was not an iconoclast. He came not to destroy, but to fulfil. He built no temple, but lived the life of simple service. He taught that the spirit was worth more than the letter; loving ministration worth more than burnt offering and bloody sacrifice.

The disciples of Christ in their effort to carry out his teachings and embody his spirit, gathered together first as friends of a mutual friend, to talk of his wonderful words and life, and to consult as to the best way of reaching others with the truth which they had received. They were simply seeking to live the life and follow the teachings of him whose disciples they were. They had no thoughts of a great organization, but lived out their lives naturally in the midst of heathenism, licentious living, and corrupt government. Thus they were forced to come together for mutual edification. Their first duties were largely social. Loss of employment on account of religion was of common occurrence, so that the little band of believers were forced to have all things in common. In carrying out the spirit of their teacher, they recognized no caste distinctions

REPRESENTING ORGANIZED RELIGION

or difference on account of position or posses-
sions. Like their teacher, they healed the sick
and cared for the needy. Because their collective life was the embodiment of the spirit
rather than of a legal institution, it touched
man in all of his relations, and was truly social in its influence.

Three great movements characterize the out-
going of religion, "Godward," "together" and
"manward." The first may be individual, as
when the human heart calls out for that which
is not of self, and recognizes the imminent God
as the deepest fact of the universe. At other
times it is social, as when by sudden impulse,
large numbers of men cry out for the living
God and the transforming power enters their
lives. Then with one accord they come together as a company of believers of like mind
and heart. If religion stops here, it will become fixed in its organization and selfish in its
life. Its only salvation is in its next step, outward and manward. The mountain-top inspiration is useless, unless the power is used
for healing in the actual touch of life. "Together" is a word full of great social significance. It means organization through the "fellowship of ministering," as in the early Church.
It also means the gentle art of living together
in the social relationships spiritualized and
made a power for good.

The early church was simple in its life, and
earnest in its purpose to bring the world into

that ideal society called the Kingdom of God—the constant theme of the teachings of Jesus. The Church was the instrument by which this wider society was to be established. It was the means of which that was the end; not an end in itself. Organized religion, as we know, was of slow growth. The Church which was formed to make it easier to minister unto men, at last came to be so strong that it forced men to minister unto it. Putting itself on the defensive, it sought to guard its riches, material and intellectual, from the attack of the sinner and the scientist.

The Church of the Middle Ages drifted far away from the simple life of Jesus. With great riches and ecclesiastical authority, it had little in common with the humble Nazarene, who had not where to lay his head. The reformed Church lived a simple life, but in placing its emphasis on individualism, it sought to save the individual rather than to transform the social life; to save a soul for eternal life, rather than to labor for the preservation and enrichment of the life that now is. This led to a dual living—a false distinction between the secular and religious, and the anomaly of saying prayers on Sunday and using false weights on Monday. With pride for certain interior moral qualities, Christian men left undone their civic, social and industrial duties. Tolstoi was not far wrong when he said that the Church, while it believes itself to be the possessor of a future life of eternal beatitude, fails too often to beautify with worthy deeds this present life.

Because organized religion has been considered largely as an institution to be defended rather than as a force for service, the united impulse for all great world movements for social reform have generally come from without. The Church has always been conservative. Witness the struggle for freedom, for temperance, and for political reform. The Church is still conservative, and therefore is not leading in the great social movement of the day. The rising power of the common man is being recognized first by Settlement and Civic Association rather than by Church and Cathedral. "Merely to attain individual morality in an age demanding social morality, is to pride one's self on the results of personal effort when the times demand social adjustment is utterly to fail to apprehend the situation."*

Referring to the subjective necessity for social settlements, Miss Addams says: "It is quite impossible for me to say in what proportion or what degree the subjective necessity which led to the opening of Hull House combined the three trends: first the desire to interpret democracy in social terms; secondly, the impulse beating at the very source of our lives urging us to aid the race in progress; and

---

*Jane Addams.

thirdly, the Christian movement toward humanitarianism." While the modern social movements are the result of the teachings of the Church, yet at present the Settlement seems to be outstripping organized religion in the very kind of social service exemplified by Jesus himself.

The great movement for civic righteousness is largely outside of organized religion. Governor Folk writes: "We are in the beginning of the greatest moral awakening America has ever known. The next four years will be distinguished as the time in which the reign of lawlessness and privilege ends and the reign of equal rights for all will become fixed in national policies and the conscience of mankind. We are entering upon the best age the world has ever known." It would almost seem that for fear of antagonizing the money interests on which its material support depends, the Church as an institution does not lead in this movement.

Organized religion is disturbed by the great social unrest, but every real student of conditions is convinced that this is a part of the great world movement upward—the cry of the soul for light and power and opportunity. The movement needs spiritual leaders, and not destroyers; men who realize that this is the breaking away from mere outward authority, caused by the application to social and industrial questions of the teachings of Jesus in the

Golden Rule and the Sermon on the Mount. As in other great movements, the Church is following where it ought to be leading. There are signs that point to the fact that the next great awakening in the Church will be a social awakening. Books on this subject are more popular than those on theology or church history. Many men, tired of formalism, are entering into social, humanitarian and reform work. Emphasis is being placed on conduct and life. Exhortations are given to do justice and love mercy, rather than to rest in a self-centered religion of emotion. The obligation of brotherhood is pressed home with increasing emphasis. Distinctions of race and education are being ignored, and the inspiring vision of the "parliament of man and the federation of the world" is becoming the hope of many. They are following George Macdonald when he says: "A man must not choose his neighbor; he must take the neighbor that God sends him. In him, whomsoever he be, lies hidden or revealed a beautiful brother. Thy neighbor is just the man who is next to you at this moment. This love of thy neighbor is the only door out of the dungeon of self."

Individual churches in trying to adapt themselves to new conditions of life, oftentimes go too far and forget that the real power is the spiritual. Here and there a church is providing some altruistic outlet for religious feeling by appointing committees to identify the church with various social lines of civic and philanthropic work. When cities have failed to open vacation schools, groups of churches have given the money and the workers for this beautiful service. In referring to this, Mr. Jacob Riis says: "The children's plight in the tenement-house region in which 'all influences make for unrighteousness,' is utterly appalling. The churches standing dark and silent on week days, were a constant reminder of our little faith, to me. You have done a lot in opening them to the children, and done it right. The blessing will not fail to follow." A writer in the Outlook, in describing a needy part of New York, says that the parish house of St. Cyprian's will be built before the church. It is hoped that there will be public baths, pool tables, reading rooms, kindergarten and accommodations for cooking and sewing. Scores of large churches have awakened out of their ecclesiastical dream and are now doing the things that the community needs to have done.

Many pastors are leading their people into social service by giving such advice as this: "This year I have come back especially impressed with the social significance of that supreme event, the Incarnation; with the duties which the life of the Divine Man shows us, we owe to each other as friends and neighbors, as partners and competitors, as employers and employed, as more favored by circumstance and Divine endowment, and less favored as brothers all, sons of one loving Father. The inward, Godward, private and personal side of religion must ever be that with which we must start. To it we must ever recur. But to stop there is to lose even that which we have. Love to God is the living root of which love to man is the growth. If the second does not appear, it is a proof that the first is dead. The great need of our day is that men would have it disclosed to them to what an extent the selfishness of our business and social life has encroached upon and strangled Christian love, and stayed the advance of the Kingdom of God upon earth."*

What the Church of the future will be, no one can predict. For the present it is clear that organized religion to be the power that it ought to be, must be socialized. The buildings must become places not for words only, but for works; to them must come the distressed and the despairing, the perplexed and the oppressed, and there find a friend in need. It must in a word become a week-day ministry to daily needs.

The unselfish life is the highest type for every day. How can a man worship in a cathedral and be happy when he knows that thousands of God's creatures are living in unhealthy tenements; that factories are destroy-

---

*W. R. Taylor, Brick Church, Rochester, N. Y.

ing life and limb, and that unnecessary disease and death exist on all sides? The call is not for more money to endow cathedrals, but for more love that touches human life.

Organized religion finds its expression Godward and manward, yet it is difficult to keep its proportionate emphasis. The tendency today is toward the Institutional Church, yet such a church is a failure unless it is also an Inspirational Church; a church of high ideals. It is a significant fact that at the time when the social conscience is being aroused, there comes the most insistent call for the spiritual life. Nor will it be satisfied with the old terms and definitions; the spiritual life demanded must be the practical, and must aid in the solution of social problems. But mountain-top inspirations are absolutely necessary. The Vision must come before the Voice. He who daily practices the presence of God is the one best fitted to lead. The constant retirement into the Holy of Holies for communion with the Spirit gives the secret of power.

From a psychological standpoint, the holding of a high ideal, the concentration of thought upon the social ideals of Jesus, will produce results that cannot be understood by the mere materialist. This is the power which can make a man immune to evil about him, and more than this, it gives him power over environment itself. Leading men to recognize the unity of all life is the quickest way to

McKINLEY INDUSTRIAL HOME FOR BOYS

bringing them into right relations to their
fellow men. The Captain of Industry, the
breaker boy at the coal mine, the bobbin girl
in the factory, are essentially and fundamen-
tally one. "Ye be of one blood, my brothers."
Once touch men's souls with this sentiment,
and the inequalities and wrongs of life will
soon disappear.

When the preacher is an inspirer to social
service, the church becomes a power house.
To such a church men will go not for dry discussion, or for the cultivation of mere aesthetic emotion, but for inspiration; for the conscious accumulation of force; for an inflow of
divine love, so that they may become co-
workers with the divine in establishing the society of Jesus. To be of the greatest service,
the minister need not drag the horrors of the
slums and the sins of men into his pulpit talk.
Literature is full of that. Better, far better,
speak of the good, the true, the beautiful, the
ideal in society and life, until men are stirred
to go forth as leaders in civic betterment and
in the movement for the city beautiful.

It is the rule of most social settlements to
pass over to the municipality all work as fast
as the city is ready to take it up. This also
ought to be the policy of Institutional
Churches. They ought to do the work that
needs to be done; healing the sick, clothing the
naked; educating, entertaining, conducting
clubs and circles, leading in the good work of

15

bettering society; making their work educational, and passing it on to the municipality just as fast as it is ready to take it up.

An Institutional Church is not simply an aggregate of institutions with stereotyped methods. Its value lies in its spirit of ministration and in its power to adapt itself to the daily needs of the entire community. The City of the Angels is a City of Churches. Every phase of religious thought is here represented, and every world religion has its following. The regular churches are many in number, well housed and strong in their influence, embracing in their membership a large proportion of the prominent and wealthy citizens—a social power which, if once combined, none of the evil forces could stand before it. But power unused, decays. Power misdirected is wasted. The division into innumerable sects is a source of great weakness. Divisions on account of non-essentials of belief are foolish and unwise. In the effort on the part of organized religion to adapt itself to changed conditions of society, there must de developed a unity of thought and effort before there can be large results in social service. The spirit of "getting together" is in the air. At last the majority of the churches has begun to federate their forces. In Los Angeles, the Church Federation includes nearly every evangelical church, and every member of the hundred or more churches included is also a member of the Federation. The Council of this organization, which meets once a month, is elected by representatives from the different churches. It includes both ministers and laymen, in about equal numbers, and practically every church with a membership of three hundred or more is represented in the Council. The Council is subdivided into eight standing committees, namely: Executive, Evangelistic, Financial, Investigation of Inter-denominational Enterprises, Parish and Canvassing, Coffee Clubs, Sunday Afternoon Popular Meetings, and Civic Righteousness.

Some of the results of this splendid union are already evident. Perfect harmony and a larger fellowship already testify to a possibility of uniting all Christian people on moral issues.

Social and municipal questions are now being thought of as important. From now on the Federation of Churches is a force to be reckoned with by the machine politicians. Christian people are coming to see that they are not merely pilgrims to another world, but citizens of this world, with power to introduce a heavenly society here and now. The movement in behalf of the young people which in the last few years has gained great momentum is being turned into practical channels along the lines of Christian citizenship. Many of the young men thus trained are entering into political life with high ideals of service.

The Christian Endeavors of the city discovered in 1903 the need of a place where men could go to pass their leisure time with opportunities for reading or playing games, and where good wholesome food could be obtained as cheaply as possible. This resulted in the opening of Coffee Club No. 1, at 133 East Second Street, which proved such a success that Coffee Club No. 2 was soon opened at 112 Court Street. Papers, magazines and games were provided for the free use of the men, and the lunch service has been increased from coffee and rolls, or doughnuts, provided at first, to a full menu. The clubs are maintained by the profits of the lunch counter. All money remaining after the current expenses have been met has been used to improve the club appointments, or to establish new ones. This Coffee Club movement was so successful that the Church Federation decided to join in this practical social service with the Coffee Club Association. In June, 1906, they opened large and beautiful rooms in the basement at Third and Main Streets. Here is a place for the young men who are strangers in the city, to become acquainted; for the young man in business who has for a home only a lonely room, to meet with his friends; a place for business men to meet in lunch hour conferences; a place for committee meetings and for the members of the Church Federation to gather and to learn to know each other better and plan for the extension and the enlargement of their work.

It is noteworthy that in few cities is there such a hearty coöperation between the Catholics and Protestants in all matters affecting public morality, as in this city. Priest and minister, Episcopal and Roman bishop are oftentimes upon the same platform, engaged in the same good work. In addition to its time-honored and noble philanthropies, the Catholic Church is using its great powers more and more in the line of general social service.

For years the Salvation Army and the Volunteers of America have been doing social as well as evangelistic work. Both are now housed in well-equipped buildings, with clinics, employment offices, clothing departments, lodgings, coffee houses and reading rooms. They are especially fitted to conserve the great social waste. Through these organizations, thousands of destitute women and children have their lives brightened by trips to the sea.

A noteworthy movement in this city is that of Christ Church, where the Men's Club have built a commodious club house which will be the gathering point for all the men who are interested in a larger life for themselves and for the city—a place where plans will be formed for turning spiritual power into practical service; where new ideas of value will be created; where people will learn that social service is more to be desired than personal gain.

In a recent description of a new undertaking for the good of the colored race, it was said that whereas the father sought to achieve personal success, the son's ideal is to achieve the success of the community. Personal holiness and social welfare cannot be separated in the teachings of the Church if organized religion is to be effective. The new professions may prove to be as sacred as the gospel ministry, and many young men who desire to be of service to the world will consecrate themselves to be city architects, sanitary engineers, superintendents of playgrounds, school gardens, coffee clubs, head workers in settlements—always on the firing line, where the victory is to be won.

The Y. M. C. A. and the Y. W. C. A. are recognized as strong factors in organized religion. They together with the Church are hearing the call of the larger social service. Through their educational classes and athletic work, they are touching large numbers of lives for good. No one can read that thrilling description of the life of the working girl portrayed in "The Long Day" without wondering if the Y. W. C. A. will not earnestly undertake to change the conditions which mean so much for so many girls. The plans for the new Y. M. C. A. building include many features which will prove of great social value. Cannot this institution become even more largely socialized? Is there not a possibility that the great centralized institution drawing individuals out of evil conditions and bad environment may be broken into smaller neighborhood groups, as far as possible, the membership working and living in these community centers, for the social and moral uplift of all young men, foreigners as well as Americans, degenerates and defectives, as well as the well born and carefully nurtured?

Among the institutions of Los Angeles most thoroughly socialized is the Bethlehem Institutional Church, or as it is now known, the Bethlehem Institutions. Mr. N. O. Nelson, the widely known philanthropist of St. Louis, speaks of it as "the best assortment of self-helping and restorative things I know of anywhere." The value of this work consists not in the great number of departments, but in the spirit which permeates all. The pastor and his family have lived in this congested district, in the midst of saloons and red-lights, for eleven years, living the life of loving service. A noble group of altruistic workers have gathered about them. All the departments of the work are the result of a normal growth, the satisfying of a pressing need. The Church is the center of all, not sectarian, but deeply spiritual, and working in perfect harmony with Hebrews and Catholics. Its ministry takes the form of a free dispensary for the suffering ones; a public bath house, the forerunner of local Municipal Baths, Coffee Clubs and Reading Rooms, open from 6 A. M. until midnight; Men's Hotels, clean homelike places where there are no rules, and no man is asked about his past life, but where everyone is expected to live as a gentleman in a large family group; halls for concerts, lectures, and as common civic centers; an industrial department where every man is put to work until employment can be obtained through the large Employment Department. There is no charity, except as one likes to help a brother. Helping men to help themselves is carried out to the full, and men are helped to be themselves, making it possible to live out their largest lives. As the neighborhood is foreign, the policy of Bethlehem to reach all the people, has led to the establishment of night schools for Spanish, Greek, Italian, Russian and Japanese in the effort to educate all into the highest citizenship.

Once a year students in Sociology from four Southern California colleges, spend a week at Bethlehem, studying with the pastor all the social conditions of the city, listening to the reports of all the leaders in reform and those who are seeking to make a better city. These students leave with a determination to make their lives count in the work of social regeneration. There are at all times students in residence, and it is to be hoped that many more will take advantage of this opportunity of

MOTHER HOUSE OF THE BETHLEHEM INSTITUTIONS

working in and with this neighborhood. A new and far-reaching educational movement has been inaugurated under the leadership of Bethlehem. The high schools in Southern California are being offered the privilege of hearing social experts on questions of social and civic import. The object of this lecture work is to familiarize those young men and women, many of whom will be leaders in city life within the next few years, with the great social problems to be met, that they may appreciate their magnitude, and be fitted to do their share toward their solution. The Bethlehem Deaconess conducts a Summer School of Social Service for women, in which students and teachers may learn to put in practice the uplifting thoughts of the school room.

In extending the Bethlehem idea, three new neighborhoods have been entered, in each of which, when the institutions are fully developed, as large work will be done as at the Mother House. As an example of unity in work and purpose, the Spanish Presbyterian Church conducts its services in the Bethlehem building, and for a year this was the meeting place for the Russian Church, known as the Brotherhood of Spiritual Christians. They are still closely allied to the Institution. The Bethlehem spirit of loving service is expressed by the poem of John G. Whittier, adopted as the Bethlehem Hymn.

"O, Brother Man, fold to thy heart thy brother!
For where love dwells, the peace of God is there,
To worship rightly is to love each other;
Each smile a hymn, each kindly deed a prayer.

"Follow with reverent steps the great example
Of Him whose holy work was doing good;
So shall the wide earth seem our Father's temple,
Each loving life, a psalm of gratitude."

The recognition of the unity of life, of the presence and power of God in the human soul, of the possibilities of development of every man, are thoughts that are stirring men's minds more and more, leading men to unite in the effort to develop the ideal society which was the dream of Jesus. Organized religion socialized will be the greatest power in making this a Better City.

CHAPTER XII.

THE OTHER FELLOW

In that beautiful oriental story of the brides-maids, told by Jesus, five were prudent, taking with them extra oil for their vessels, ready for an emergency. When the bridegroom came they were the only ones prepared to enter in. "They that were ready went in." Opportunity does not make the man; it reveals him. Doors open to prepared ones. They that are ready may enter into the kingdom of nature, art, music, literature or love.

There is great danger in this commercial age that the only preparation may be to enter into the Kingdom of Money. If the higher interests of life are neglected in youth, then in after years the doors that lead into the higher spiritual realms will be shut. Andrew Carnegie's word ought to be accepted as truth when he says: "Money does not make a man happy. I would give up all the wealth I have rather than be denied the pleasures that come from the study of literature and art. If Shakespeare and Wagner, the mountain peaks of literature and music, were taken out of my life, life would be very poor indeed. Millionaires who live mostly for making money have a sorry time of it in comparison with the possibilities of the life they might live." In a more recent address, he reveals the fact that his mind is being drawn even more strongly to the spiritual ideals. He said, referring to his own city :* "There is room for many things of the spirit in our city. Things material are abundant, our mills and factories numerous, large and prosperous; but things material, including money itself, should be only the foundation upon which are reared things spiritual. Our mines of coal and iron have not completed their mission when transmitted into articles for use, and these into dollars. All is still on the material plane. Not till the dollars are transmuted into service for others in one of the many forms best calculated to appeal to and develop those higher things of the moral, intellectual and aesthetic domain, has wealth completely justified its existence. Dollars are only dross until spiritualized, a means to an end; and miserable is the man, mean and squalid his life, who knows no better than to deaden his soul by mere possession, counting over a hoard which holds him down, or using his faculties in old age in augmenting the useless stuff that ministers not to any taste worthy of man."

The altruistic spirit is not a miraculous gift, but rather the result of daily thoughts and daily deeds. Looking out for one's self will

---

*Pittsburg.

never enable a person to look out for the interests of the other fellow. But he who does a kind deed today is preparing to enter into the kingdom of love and service tomorrow. The priest and the Levite in the gospel story were very religious, yet when the opportunity came to them of helping the man in need, they were not ready, but passed by on the other side. Living only in the kingdom of formal religious observance, they were not able to enter into the larger kingdom of loving service.

The world today needs the good Samaritan —the man with the altruistic spirit in his breast for the other fellow, whether he be prisoner, tramp, working man or capitalist. Because of the rapid increase of this spirit in the hearts of men, we can but be hopeful for the coming age. The object of this chapter is to bring home to each reader the thought of his own responsibility to the other fellow, and to show what he can do to help him to rise out of his poverty, his vice and his ignorance. Experience has shown that in helping another to help himself, we at the same time help ourselves.

An apostle of old once said in substance: "If a brother or sister be hungry or naked and you say, 'God bless you, I hope that you will find warmth and food,' what does it profit you?" If anyone is to be truly helpful to another who is in need, there must be a personal touch, a real exhibition of friendship. Henry Clay Trumbull has well described the meaning of friendship: "It consists in loving rather than in being loved, in being a friend rather than in having a friend; in giving our affection unselfishly and unswervingly to another—not in being the object of another's affections." "Love reckoneth not up her wrongs," but continues to work with the needy one though he be both unlovely and ungrateful. It is one of the axioms of the science of charity, that relief must be sympathetic. Nothing short of personal human sympathy and kindness have in them healing power.

Of late we have had many exhibitions of world-wide sympathy, showing that the hearts of men are ringing true to the best that is in them. Abundant relief has been sent to the famine-stricken in India, Japan and China. But it remained for the dreadful calamity which befell the city by the Golden Gate to show in what a full-hearted measure men can at times think and act unselfishly. The ethical gain through this outpouring of money and food and personal service has been greater by far than any material loss. The calamity set in motion a tidal wave of helpful sympathy which swept around the world. Many who for the first time discovered the pleasure of giving themselves in personal service, will never cease in their good works, but will become permanent factors in the social uplift of the world. In every city there is an increasing group of those who are altruistic, deeply spiritual, and moved by the power of the social passion. They are intensely interested in the "man with the hoe" and in "those without the camp." In olden times the leper was driven without the camp to exist as best he could until death brought relief. Today men of Father Damiens' type are living beside them with a helpful ministry; and better still, noble-hearted individuals, devoted to the healing art, are seeking to find the cause and the cure of the dreadful plague. Nor is it enough to drive the moral leper without the camp. The philanthropist of the present must study the cause and the cure of the vice and crime which are such a hindrance to the moral progress of society, so as to put things right at the fountain head.

Making man fit to survive is far better than trusting to the operation of the evolutionary law of the survival of the fittest. The strong animal drives the weakling to the wall, but in a strong man there ought to be developed the God-like attribute of devoting his best effort to defend the weak one. The thought of getting together for the purpose of being mutually helpful as brothers all, may seem to many as almost Utopian, yet it is growing, and the progress toward this ideal is so rapid that there ought to be few doubters left as to the final outcome.

In the industrial world fortunes are now being made from the by-products which come from what was formerly discarded. In the great abattoirs, nothing is lost. The old dump heap at the smelter is now worth more than the product of many mines. The refuse picked from the street sweepings goes far toward paying the expenses of cleaning New York's streets. Now if this seeming material waste is of so much value, is there not social value to be redeemed from our great social waste? Read any of the recent descriptive books telling how the other half lives; visit Whitechapel in London, or the slums of our great cities, and answer for yourself the question whether there is not a far greater loss of social values than would ever be permitted in the industrial life. Is not a man better than a sheep? And is not a redeemed man better than the by-product of a factory? The captains of industry employ trained scientists and experts to transform waste into value, yet until recently little has been done with the social waste of the world. The city and the nation ought to employ noted sociologists and trained experts to bring forth value from social waste. When the mighty call came for help from the stricken city of San Francisco, the President was quick to act in sending noted specialists to aid in the great work or rehabilitation. And may we not hope that there will soon be inaugurated a new department of government

LOS ANGELES COUNTY POOR FARM

service, composed of sociological experts, who shall be placed upon an equality with the Department of Commerce, and that every city shall have its Superintendent of Social Service, trained in mind and in heart for the great work of social uplift. In the matter of taking account of moral values, New Zealand is far ahead in the great social work of the world. It has made taxpayers out of tramps and fellow citizens out of slum dwellers. Happily, interest in the human wreckage of the world is now being aroused. On every hand we find the tramps, the beach combers of society, the out-of-works who have been made such because of the changed industrial conditions; the drunkard, the product of the American saloon; the prisoners separated from the touch of society; the scarlet woman scorned by her sisters; the pauper who has dropped forever below the line of self-support and self-respect; and having seen these, the great heart of the world can never again rest at ease in its luxury and wealth. Men are bound together by heart strings. "No man liveth to himself." "Each for all and all for each" is the guiding rule in the ideal society which is to be. Today we are separated into castes and classes. There is the great gulf between the master and servant, rich and poor, learned and ignorant, good and bad. Men are sons of a common Father, but not brothers all, or at least their brotherhood is not yet actualized. This condition

16

cannot long obtain, for it is evident to all that progress of society is not by the advance of the exceptional men, but by the gradual uplift of the helpless and the weak; it is in the forward march of the masses, and not in the progress made by an elect few. You and I, my brother, will truly rise in the world not by rising upon our fellows or above them, but by seeking their mutual uplift and taking them along with us. No man should ever go slumming out of curiosity, for the dwellers in our slums are not like strange creatures in a menagerie; they are but weak and neglected brothers, for whose condition we may be in part responsible; we are therefore to go down to them into the darkness in which they live, searching for the good and not for the bad, endeavoring to call out the best that is in them. In that spirit we are to go into the jails and police courts and look upon the wreck and ruin wrought by sin; into the filthy tenements where the squalor and disease abide; go into the groggery and barrel house where men and women are sunk in debauchery; into the lower regions of the demimonde where men and women are sunk beneath the beasts; into the gambler's den where men entice the young to their ruin or enchain them in a fearful habit from which they cannot free themselves; and when the horror of all this has taken hold of your heart, you will be the first to join the noble rank of reformers; and you will learn to have more sympathy with rescue workers and Salvation Army lasses as they toil and pray that a few may be brought out of that wretchedness and misery into a better life. The gentle white-capped women caring for those who are dying in a hospital broken through dissipation and defilement, will also appear to you like Angels of Mercy sent to a sin-cursed world.

Ye men who are living soft, easy lives, thinking only of self and family, is it not time to begin to think of the other fellow? Is it not worth while to live so that it may be said of you what was said of one of the noblest men as they laid him away, "He was a great-hearted and true-hearted man. He cared not for riches and station. He rose far above distinctions and divisions. He was a friend and a brother of men. His heart was large enough for all the people. The friend of man, the friend of the weary and worn, the weakest and the worst."* The glory of this man lay not in the fact that he was a captain of industry, but in the fact that he was a loving brother to every man.

The lift of every man's heart is upward; to help another human soul in its upward evolution is life's greatest and most joyful privilege; to lend ourselves each to the other as an inspiration to grander living is life's highest ministry and reward.

---

*Samuel M. Jones, Toledo.

Do you say that these sentiments may sound well? Yes, but they would appear still better if applied to all conditions of life. Consider for instance, what would be the result if they were applied to the man who has broken the laws of the land. The prisoner is for the most part a good man gone wrong, and by proper treatment is capable of redemption. Only about ten per cent of the inmates of our jails and penitentiaries may be considered as real criminals, but are brought to their condition by bad environment, bad parentage, physical malformation, or weak will. According to the old idea of retributive punishment, the law breaker must feel the full vengeance of society for the crime he had committed. It was fancied that this would deter him from future crimes and be a warning to others. But such has not been the result of the age-long system of retributive punishment. The man who has been in prison is more likely to offend again. The man who is a law breaker is still a man and like us needs a friend and helpful surroundings. The best of men would receive harm if herded together in a common jail. The psychological effect would be harmful to the entire man. In a recent report on prisons, a writer says: "There is need of hope for every individual. If you send a man to the county jail or put him in prison for a fixed term, hope is gone, the stigma of prison is upon him; the long blank years are before him; he is conscious more or less that he is on the way toward becoming a worse man; he gives himself up to his destiny and abandons himself to a riot of bad intentions and evil thoughts. Keep his hope alive; keep him out of prison, under the charge of a probation officer; let him feel that if he behaves himself, he may return back in freedom to his natural surroundings without ever having entered prison. At the same time, fear must go hand in hand with hope; he must be made to feel that if he fails, prison life is the result. The probation law provides just these possibilities. When the judge sees fit to give a man another chance, he has all the help that a kind probation officer can give him, and above all, he is kept away from the prison associations. This system has been so successful with child delinquents, it is surprising that it is not more often resorted to in the case of adults. In the light of dollars and cents, it pays to reform a prisoner, rather than to keep him locked up in a prison whose methods may only deform him. The treatment of the criminal today ought to be reformative rather than punitive. This is a principle only partially carried out in any California city. The truant officer looks after the boys and girls who are not in school, and places them in the truant school. If brought before the Juvenile Court, the Probation officer becomes responsible to the Court for their conduct. The reform school is used only as a last resort, and in this state it is rapidly being depopulated. The record thus far shows that the truant officer, and the parental school, return seventy-five or eighty per cent back on the right track, to remain there. The Juvenile Court is credited with an equally high per cent. What next? The prisons? No, it is the reformatory. When criminals under thirty-five are given a chance to make a good record for themselves, seventy-five per cent of these can be returned to their home and friends better, or at least not worse for their experience. The incorrigible remainder are the only ones that the penitentiary ought to claim. A reformatory is a place of hope, for by good conduct and study and work every man may cut short his sentence and become proficient as an apprentice in several trades. A man with a five-year sentence may by good conduct regain his freedom in one year.

In Massachusetts most of the habitual drunkards under thirty-five are sent to the reformatory for a year and a day, rather than subjected to the method employed in most states, which does not aid these men in the recovery of their normal life. Such unfortunates ought to be considered diseased and sent to a farm, where by work, good fresh air, and pleasant surroundings they could be made strong in body and in will power, and able to meet the temptation which society places in their way.

Too great emphasis cannot be laid upon man's duty to his fellow man who has fallen by the way. More money, more thought, and more personal service should be expended on him, for is he not our brother? Yet after all has been done that it is possible to do in this way, it is not enough, for there are causes which must be removed before there can be any great gain. Rescue workers feel that they are standing at the foot of a cliff picking up a few of the many who have been thrown over and have fallen at their feet, healing them and starting them upward, some of them to be thrown over again and again. Better put a fence at the top and change the forces which make for destruction.

It is not always easy to decide where to put the stress of our labor for the good of humanity. Because individual sin and wretchedness and misery press so closely upon us, we are led to feel that the greatest thing in the world is to fit the socially disabled ones to take their place in the ranks of the independent. The teacher, the preacher, the rescue worker are seeking to give strength to the weak will, that there may be the power within to resist the evil. But there are social causes which make for dependency and crime that are beyond the control of the individual. It is the growing belief that expending our effort upon results is not enough, but that our main effort must be directed toward the destruction of the social causes for the spiritual wreckage. In this way alone will permanent help come to those who cannot help themselves—the child, the sick, the man with a weak will. The doing of kindly deeds for the poor that we may have peace of mind and a pleasant sense of duty well done has its origin not in an altruistic but a selfish impulse. The sentiment, "Throw out the life line," is not enough. Go to the bathing beaches and see a better life line—one stretched out into the surf where thousands of bathers can disport themselves without fear of drowning. "Put out the life line—mend the broken rail, destroy the saloon, brothel and gambling den, make and enforce laws against child labor, which is making the 'hoe man.' Prosecute the makers of impure foods and medicines, destroy the tenements and rookeries, replacing them with decent homes. Stand for a living wage for all men. These are a few of the causes of the crime and dependency with which we are all so familiar."

In a recent paper on housing conditions in Los Angeles, a member of the Housing Commission reported the terrible conditions existing at that time on Utah Street, where over 400 Mexicans lived in shacks crowded in one small block. Many of these he reported as keeping their tiny houses clean and their children neatly clad, and trying their best to make a home. Were it not for causes beyond their control, they would have a home in pleasant

"PUT OUT THE LIFE LINE"

surroundings.   These particular people were imported as cheap labor from Mexico.   They do not receive a living wage, and so are forced to live in this congested manner, productive of sickness and crime.   Who pays in the end when less than a living wage is given by the corporation?   First the laborer and his family by the loss of physical and moral strength; second, the public who must through taxes meet the cost of extra jails for those made criminals by this congestion, and who must provide for the care of the sick in the public hospitals, and possibly bear the expense of fighting the contagion which may spread from this street throughout the city.   Some one must pay the bills.   Who pays the bills when the laborer is maimed for life?   Not the employer, but the public.   It is easy to see that to help the other fellow means more than a daily dole.   Modern philanthropy must go to the source whence dependency originates, and work there with causes.   Judge Lindsey is quoted as saying: "The Juvenile Court stands second; it handles results: the Juvenile Association first; it removes causes.   The suggestion of a state department for the elimination of crime is worthy of serious attention, if through that the causes of crime may be studied and faithfully dealt with."

The ablest lawyers are retained in the service of vested interests, whose duty it is to see that not one dollar is lost to employers by the passage and enforcement of laws for the safety and health of the common people. Thus the passage of the pure food laws was delayed many years; thousands of unsanitary tenements were left untouched and laws against the sale of liquor and of cigarettes to minors are made dead letters. Is it not then a matter of necessity that the ablest experts be employed by the people to study conditions that make for these evils; suggest better laws and attend to their enforcement; in other words, stand between the people and the employers' greed for gold; be the educators of the new generation of philanthropists; be the forerunners of the day when the word "People" will be written in larger letters than the word "King" or "Priest" or "Captain of Industry."

By way of summary, let it be noted that the Associated Charities has more to do than to tabulate cases; the Merchants' and Manufacturers' Association must go deeper than the ferreting out of frauds; the philanthropic societies must do more than care for the products of an evil system; the Church must learn that the power of religion has only been half applied. All these organizations must stand for the new Civic Spirit. They must busy themselves in studying the tenement problem; in calling the attention of public authorities to homes that are unfit; in studying the best methods of sanitation; in doing their part toward the destruction of the great white plague, tuberculosis. "Sanitation is a social problem; public health is a social problem. If there be a disease in the slum and a breeze sweeps over the city, disease is everywhere. After that there are no slums and there are no safe quarters, for no city is better, either morally or physically, than its worst part." If no state can exist half slave and half free, it may more truly be said that no city can live half good and half bad. Left to itself, the slum will breed the criminal, who will rob or burn the mansion in the finer district. One garment made in a sweat shop may contaminate with disease a healthy family in the beautiful suburban home. The uneducated foreigner, the prey of the politician, may help to install vicious men in office who will destroy the fair name of a city and set back progress for many years. Experience dearly bought is teaching the truth of the words that "no man liveth to himself and no man dieth to himself." Let us ask what shall be our attitude toward the other fellow. The Master of men answered it by saying, "Thou shalt love thy neighbor as thyself." Not more, not less. That which you desire for yourself or family you must wish for every man—money, friends, home, education, position, pleasant surroundings, a spiritual religion, health, happiness. Loving thy neighbor as thyself surely means that you are to desire for him, and will help him to obtain all these things, which to you make life worth living.

The coming man will be the man whose chief thought will be the upbuilding of the social kingdom; "he will move in the power of the social passion," and that is an inward propelling power, never satisfied with present attainment, but seeking for a closer touch with the divine power and the application of that power to other needs. Ever in the pursuit of the common good, he will recognize wealth as a common inheritance and living the life of loving service will be to him like partaking of the holy sacrament.

The City of the Angels is as yet far away from the ideal city. The dollar still rules. Material things are still more sought for than spiritual. Low political ideals still hold sway. Nevertheless, the brighter day is dawning. Investigation has brought forth protest and a few noble souls are leading on in the campaign for purity, temperance, righteousness and justice. There is a growing multitude who are determined that there shall be here not only a great, but a Better City.

————END————

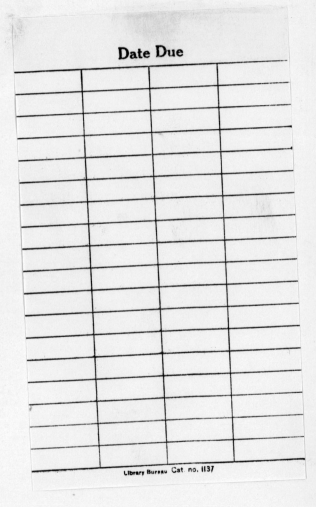

Date Due